D0349404

Macmillan Building and Surveying Series

List continued overleaf

List continued from previous page

Macmillan Building and Surveying Series
Series Standing Order
ISBN 0–333–71692–2 hardcover
ISBN 0–333–69333–7 paperback
(outside North America only)

You can receive future titles in this series as they are published by placing a
standing order. Please contact your bookseller or, in the case of difficulty, write
to us at the address below with your name and address, the title of the series
and the ISBN quoted above.

Customer Services Department, Macmillan Distribution Ltd
Houndmills, Basingstoke, Hampshire RG21 6XS, England

Property Management

A Customer Focused Approach

Gordon Edington

Foreword by Sir John Egan

MACMILLAN

First published 1997 by
MACMILLAN PRESS LTD
Houndmills, Basingstoke, Hampshire RG21 6XS
and London
Companies and representatives
throughout the world

ISBN 0-333-67470-7

A catalogue record for this book is available from the British Library.

This book is printed on paper suitable for recycling and made from fully
managed and sustained forest sources.

10   9   8   7   6   5   4   3   2
06   05   04   03   02   01   00   99   98

Printed and bound in Great Britain by
Antony Rowe Ltd Chippenham, Wiltshire

The proceeds from the sale of this book are used to support

The BAA 21st Century Communities Trust
Registered Charity Number: 1058617

The BAA Trust was established in 1996 with a remit from BAA plc to help
communities around each of its airports (Heathrow, Gatwick, Stansted,
Southampton, Glasgow, Edinburgh and Aberdeen) meet the challenge of the
21st century.

Contents

Foreword

This is an important book because property is a key industry; if it fails to be customer orientated it will also provide poor leadership for the construction industry, which desperately needs to adopt such an approach itself. The two industries, property and construction, must both focus on the needs of their customers if they are to fulfil their vital roles in any economy which aspires to be world class.

Many of those in the property business are deeply imbued with the practices of an industry which has traditionally viewed the tenant as someone whose requirements must be held in check by vigorous use of the law. I remember that when BAA plc started its company-wide 'customer-friendly' management overhaul I mentioned our desire, as a landlord, to 'satisfy our customers' to the Managing Director of one of Britain's largest property companies. He drew in his breath sharply as though this was a dangerous precedent that could cause him and his industry much harm!

This book explains how to make the transformation from a conventional property management business to one that adopts quality management practices. At the heart of the book is a description of BAA plc's Property Challenge, a model that has been used to transform a business, with not only sceptical customers but sceptical employees as well, into one that is competitive and sustainable – truly world class.

The strong theme throughout the book is how tenants should be valued as customers. Gordon has covered the subject comprehensively and the arguments put forward are well supported by case studies from the UK and USA. Cartoons add a light and humorous touch.

Global competition is going to affect all businesses and property is no excception. Change is on the way and this book suggests a step-by-step approach for the property industry facing up to the first challenge of any businesss; how to survive by being prepared for the future. Gordon has described the formula for success and in the final chapter has given some important and interesting pointers for the future.

I strongly recommend this excellent book which is likely to mark the turning point for an important and valuable industry. This book gives the opportunity for a new start where landlords can work in a spirit of true partnership with tenants and thereby add value and gain value.

SIR JOHN EGAN

ix

Preface

Property management is a business like any other. It can help to create wealth by adding value to other businesses, or at worst it can hinder and frustrate companies and detract from their competitiveness. Whether you call it property or real estate, land and buildings play a central role in a country's economic well-being. Land provides the foundations on which organizations can develop their businesses and generate prosperity.

Within the property sector, property management is often seen as the poor relation of development, yet a well-managed estate can be the springboard for the development of new buildings. Growing a business is much easier from a secure base of satisfied customers, who after all are hard to secure but easy to lose. For a property company seeking to expand there should be no other approach than one that treats tenants as a prized asset.

Despite the common sense to this approach, the management of property is often outdated and characterized by an adversarial relationship with fast recourse to the law in the event of disagreement. This is time-consuming and expensive, and in the long run will ensure that both landlord and tenant underperform in their respective businesses.

Consider the car manufacturing industry. It is today a global business, but not many years ago home markets were dominated by products from local plants. With few exceptions, that is how the property management business remains, but with accelerating globalization facilitated by technology that must change. Tenants will be more footloose and expect more for less; in essence a higher quality service at a lower cost. That is exactly what most customers want when they walk into a shop or step on to an aeroplane. Why should property be different?

Tenants will want a landlord to demonstrate that the rent represents fair value for money. They will expect choice and flexibility in the length and terms of leases, productivity deals on service charges and landlord performance targets with financial penalties. Today's way of doing things will not be good enough tomorrow. Tomorrow's tenants will require and have the right to expect the highest standards of service from their landlords. For property owners who do not rise to this challenge and who fail to adopt a world-class approach, the long-term outlook is bleak.

This book suggests a new way of working, in essence a simple common-sense approach that turns its back on the old way of treating tenants primarily as a source of upwardly mobile income. The new way recognizes that it is the tenants that are mobile and that their custom must be earned. The challenge is how to win tenants' loyalty and the starting point must be a firm belief that tenants are valued customers. This customer-driven approach will be more profitable, more sustainable and, as an important by-product, more enjoyable.

This book shares knowledge gained from practical experience. It provides managers, property professionals and all those training for a property sector career with a property management philosophy that focuses on adding value to tenants' businesses. There is theory in this book but, perhaps more importantly, an explanation of how that theory has been put into practice in BAA plc through the company's Property Challenge programme.

At its heart, the strategy is about the benefits of treating tenants as valued customers. Traditional thinking on property management gives no glimpse of the notion that if a supplier (the landlord) is receiving substantial sums (rents) from the customer (tenant), then the customer has the right to expect exemplary service. Indeed, current textbooks focus on which laws and legal cases can be used to help landlords maintain their income. A recourse to law should not be considered as somehow par for the course, but a regrettable move that endangers a valuable customer–supplier relationship.

The book explains how to go about managing this change in one of the most traditional sectors of business. The step-by-step approach is also applicable in other industries faced with a need to focus more sharply on delivering good service and good value.

Few graduates can expect to remain in one industry all their careers; the world is moving too fast. Yet the property sector has been poor at training and developing managers so that they have transferable skills that make them attractive to other industries.

This book describes the skills and processes necessary to establish a modern property management business and these elements are equally applicable to any industries: research; service to the customer; process improvement; leadership; measurement; benchmarking; and marketing. The essential need to add value to all stakeholder groups is also a recurring theme.

The essence of this book is about treating tenants as valued customers by providing them with good service and value. The logic of the philosophy is that in return tenants will deliver a more valuable income stream because, rather than taking flight at the first opportunity, they will wish to remain with a landlord who works with them in a spirit of partnership, not confrontation.

I hope this book plays a small part in helping to ensure the sustainability of property owning businesses and, equally importantly, the careers of the people who work in them.

GORDON EDINGTON

Acknowledgements

This book is firmly based on the learning that I and my colleagues at BAA plc have gained from managing the change necessary to create a customer focused property management business.

Each chapter, in essence, encapsulates a part of the company's strategic approach to property management, and is based on the experiences of managers with a particular knowledge of that part of the business. I would therefore like to acknowledge the contributions made by the following and the people who have worked with them in helping implement BAA plc's Property Challenge: Eric Armstrong, Jeremy Boyes, Peter Clegg, Terry Currion, John Herbert, Robert Herga, Guy Holden, Barry Horrell, Paul Le Marquand, John O'Halloran, John Speakman, Jonathan Strong and Tony West.

I would also like to thank others who have contributed to this book in one way or another: Georgina Allinson, William Babtie, Robert Best, Emma Boulby, Stephen Bradley, Jim Brophy, Arif Chandoo, Sheila Clark, Andrea Davis, Jatinder Dhanoa, Phil Dunn, Liz Eden, Sarah Gallagher, Jane Hart, Peter Holden, Katie Hughes, Albert Kraft, Yve Lear, Simon Macdonagh, Janet Morris, Julie Morrison, Sandra Percival, Karen Poirier, Geoffrey Reid, Philip Ross, Christine Stewart, Deborah Thomas, Mike Toms, Liz Tooke, Paul Warner, Charlotte Webb, Alastair Welch and Des Wilson.

I wanted to include case studies showing how the customer focused approach can succeed and am grateful to Barry Gibson, the Group Retail Director of BAA plc, and to his colleague Nick Ziebland, for the Airport Retailing case study in Chapter 11. I am grateful to four of my other colleagues at BAA plc, Simon Murray and Graham Matthews for their input on construction, and Alan Osborne and Tony Ryan for their advice respectively on safety and training issues.

I am also indebted to Mike Lipsey of the Lipsey Company for adding an international perspective by providing information for the American case studies in Chapter 12. In the early days when we were formulating BAA plc's property strategy, Mike was also invaluable in helping me to believe that what looked like hopelessly challenging targets were achievable – as indeed they turned out to be.

I would also like to thank John Lowry for his contribution on how information technology plays a central role in improving management performance, and to him as well as Wendy Melotte for helping me to manage the process of writing this book and for finding answers to my endless stream of queries. I am also indebted to Howard Morgan who, as well as contributing to the book, in his role of Assistant Group Property Director at BAA plc brought insight and clarity of thinking to the creation and implementation of BAA plc's Property Challenge strategy.

Thanks are also due to Erik Brown and Vic Wyman for editing the text, to Andrew Morgan for his research work and to my secretary Nickie Dean for all her good humour and commitment when faced almost daily with my revisions. I would also like to acknowledge the assistance of David Knight of Lovell White Durrant who provided valuable research for the first chapter and to Alan White for his thoughts about the future. Thanks are due to George Gale for creating the cartoons in this book and to Mark Goyder, Director, The Centre for Tomorrow's Company, for his Tomorrow's Company Inquiry research, which has been an important influence.

I thought a good first step, before starting to write this book, would be to learn from potential readers about their likes and dislikes – they were my potential customers after all! This research into the style of the book was extremely helpful and I would like to acknowledge the time spent, and guidance given, by City University Business School Department of Property Valuation and Management (Andrew Axcell, third year undergraduates and postgraduates), De Montfort University, Leicester (Elizabeth S.J. Carter and third year undergraduates and postgraduates) and the University of Reading Department of Land Management and Development (Virginia A. Gibson and third year undergraduates and postgraduates).

During much of my career I worked with Peter Olsberg and Maurice Lambert and was influenced by, and benefited greatly from, their wisdom, support and friendship.

I would also like to thank Sir John Egan, for the support he has given me in writing this book and for sharing his infectious enthusiasm for leaving no stone unturned in an effort to satisfy even the most demanding customer.

Finally, I would also like to thank my youngest son Jack for his hours of patience and forbearance in leaving me in peace when I was writing at home.

GORDON EDINGTON

1 Property Traditions

The automobile is a little over 100 years old, the wheel several thousand years old, but property and concepts of property ownership have been around since the dawn of civilization. Who is to say that Neolithic man did not allow a member of his tribe to share his cave in return for a haunch of venison each week?

Many influences have shaped the character of property rights, including economic needs, custom, history, religion and politics. Indeed, the very way in which land has been allocated and held has usually constituted one of the fundamental aspects of a culture, not least because this control has often formed the basis of economic, social and political power. Today, with the possible exception of communist regimes, land continues to represent a major source of wealth and power.

Cheshire and Burn's *Modern Law of Real Property* notes that in earlier times, in general:

> Land constituted the sole form of wealth and it was through its agency that everyday needs of the governing and the governed classes were satisfied. The result of this was that from an early date, a complicated system of law, founded on custom and developed by decisions of the courts began to grow up and we may call it for convenience the common law system.[1]
>
> (Cheshire and Burn, *Modern Law of Real Property*, 1994)

This system applies in the UK, most former British colonies and the USA. In much of Europe land tenure is based on civil codes, many from the Napoleonic times.

There is so much history and custom attached to the ownership and occupation of property that it is hardly surprising that the actual framework within which property is managed today and the relationship between landlord and tenant has been heavily influenced by ancient practices, many originating in the mists of time. This chapter will provide a brief overview of the history of land ownership, possession and occupation, and will set out some of the historical background to the traditional attitudes which pervade property management.

It is interesting first to consider the earliest socio-economic systems to look at how land tenure has evolved.

NOMADIC SOCIETY

Nomads did not stay in one place long enough to justify ownership and possession of land, whether by individuals or tribes.

Over time nomadic groups began to treat some territories as theirs by right and might defend their right to exclusive occupation against intruders, particularly where the land provided good hunting or grazing. Even so, claims for exclusive periodic occupation were for the benefit of whole tribes rather than individuals.

EARLY SETTLEMENTS

From these early settlements right up until the industrial revolution, agriculture was the primary basis for the acquisition of land. As nomadic groups turned to farming, the need grew for the individual who planted crops to be able to tend and harvest them. This was the genesis of the earliest concepts of possession and ownership of land.

Patterns of ownership developed unevenly. Migrants from the lowlands began to grow corn along the south coast of England; however, in relation to the rest of the country:

> the interior was peopled by wild tribes, all but ignorant of husbandry wandering from pasturage to pasturage with their stunted flocks or herds and living chiefly on milk and flesh.[2]
>
> (Brodrick, *English Land and English Landlords, 1881; repr. 1968*)

It seems likely that the British chiefs initially had little interest in land other than the hunting grounds and clearings of their respective tribes. Custom dictated that these lands were owned communally, there was no absolute possession, the community came first, the individual second. Eventually, as concepts of ownership grew, chiefs began to claim land as a source of wealth.

THE ROMAN SYSTEM

Though England was never entirely subdued by the Romans, the permanence of their influence is remarkable. Under the Pax Roman (Salway, 1981), the population of Britain grew rapidly and at the peak of the Roman period in 200AD the population was about 4 to 6 million.[3]

The Roman writer Tacitus noted that the Britons adopted the Roman way of life at an early stage of their long history. Under Roman rule a highly structured ownership system was introduced and large tracts of land were taken into individual or group ownership. Domains of previous rulers were annexed as State domains and these became the Emperor's personal estates administered by his nominees. These estates were frequently enlarged to include the lands of individuals or communities who resisted annexation.

On discharge from the army, soldiers often held land by grant from the authorities. Similarly the settlements founded in Britain often made land-grants to their members. These settlements often controlled territoria, that is lands subject to taxation by the city in question.

In addition to grants and annexures, there was also room for the itinerant capitalists attracted by the fertile soil to purchase land. There is evidence that there was in Britain:

> vacant land to be taken up on favourable terms, either in complete proprietor-ship or by favourable empyteutic lease, i.e., a lease which became permanent after nominal payment and conscientious cultivation for a defined period (e.g. five years).[4]   (Finberg, *Agrarian History of England*, 1, 1972)

The Romans clearly had highly developed concepts of personal ownership. There is also evidence to support the existence of contracts for the hiring of land, particularly in the towns; however, a more common picture was that of large estates of land owned individually or by the state, and worked by servants or slaves.

From 200 AD onwards the size of the population dwindled as the Roman Empire slowly declined. There is increasing evidence of abandoned land and of a severe shortage of labour. Roman leaders attempted to deal with this problem in various ways from the third century right up until the end of the Empire.

THE ANGLO-SAXON SYSTEM

There is much academic debate as to the extent to which Roman law survived and was adopted into Anglo-Saxon law following the arrival of Angles, Saxons and Jutes in the mid fifth century. It is clear however that the invaders continued to encourage private ownership, albeit on a more hierarchical basis.

Modern research shows that the Britons, far from being exterminated, outnumbered the conquerors and that:

> The Anglo-Saxons were not town dwellers and, indeed, hated towns. The survival of a number of Roman towns points to the fact that the Saxons permitted the British to continue to develop their own towns and left them much to themselves.[5]
> (Kiralfy, *Potter's Historical Introduction to English Law and its Institutions*, 1962)

The oldest type of tenure in Anglo-Saxon England was folk-land, a system of customary landholding by a family group. Under this system there was no superior landowner. The land was inalienable from that family group, being held collectively for their own common good.

The second type of ownership (Maitland, 1897) was much more influenced by Roman and Christian ideas of individual ownership and was known as book-land. This was invariably a gift from a superior, and the gift took the form of a written charter. Originally, these were made exclusively to ecclesiastics and when they were later adapted for use by others they still retained a fictional ecclesiastical guise.[6]

The last type of structure was known as laen-land which was a derivative form of landholding and originally was merely a loan of land for a life or lives with three lives being common.

From these structures, we can begin to see how the early forms of feudalism began to develop into a system where great men held their lands by book or charter from the king, and others were held from these great men by laen.

THE FEUDAL SYSTEM

The foundation of traditional and, in most cases, current landlord and tenant relationships, particularly in the UK, is the feudal system. This existed in France to a greater or lesser extent right up until the French Revolution and in the UK even longer, until the reforms of the 1920s.

Feudalism is a vague and imprecise term. The word itself derives from the late Latin 'feodum' or 'feudum' meaning a fife or fee. Fees were in origin the grant of land made to a man in return for service. The system developed in Europe out of the anarchy and barbarism which resulted from the decline of the Roman Empire and from the needs of small tenants or landowners to gain protection from outside attack by enemies, intruders or simply other more powerful landowners.

Feudalism developed into an administrative and judicial system as well as giving entitlement to land. That entitlement did not confer ownership -- merely possession. Stubbs, in his *Constitutional History of England*, described the fully developed system as one 'based on land tenure in which every lord judged, taxed and commended the class next below him'.[7] At each level, there was a communal benefit in the protection of the inferior by the superior against invaders and aggressive neighbours greedy for more land.

Although feudalism continued to develop in a haphazard way within the British Isles, it only really took hold following the Norman invasion, when William claimed title to the whole of England and with it the power to redistribute the land. This he proceeded to do, granting large tracts of conquered Saxon lands to his Norman supporters in return for payments and other services. Later monarchs continued to exercise the power of confiscation coupled with the grant of lands in return for favours. Even now there is a presumption in the UK of ownership by the Crown unless there is evidence that land is owned by someone else.

Feudal landholding was based on the superiority of owners and possessors of land over those to whom rights were granted. Tenure existed only as long as the subservient holder provided the dominant lord with the agreed services or dues. If they ceased to be provided, the dominant lord could seize the tenant's goods to force payment and, ultimately, evict the tenant and grant the land to someone else. In England, the dues could be of any nature, military, financial or personal. In the rest of Europe the grant of land was almost always in return for military service.

In the early stages of the feudal system, a tenant could not recover land of which he was wrongly dispossessed and could only seek damages against the landlord for breach of covenant. Bad landlords could demand extortionate rents and had absolute power to evict tenants. Because the landlord was probably the judge in the court that heard any claim for damages for wrongful eviction, the tenant was unlikely to receive a fair hearing.

From about 1235 in England tenants were able to bring actions to recover land or property, but only against the original landlord or their successors. It was not until the second half of the fifteenth century that the courts allowed tenants to recover land from any wrongful claimant and to claim damages.

In the struggle between king and parliament culminating in the Civil War, the existence of feudal revenues enabled the king to avoid summoning parliament as he had no need for parliamentary taxes. Accordingly, when parliament did eventually meet, it set about abolishing feudal dues in a number of Acts, leading up to the Tenures Abolition Act 1660. This Act finally abolished military tenures in England and any remaining military service became honorary and therefore largely ceremonial. This Act left two distinct forms of tenure – common socage (freehold) and copyhold. Since 1660 the rights of the lord of freehold land have been of little significance, because under these tenures no special services were due and no special customs applied.

Copyhold emerged from the feudal system of villeinage under which servants were given sufficient land to till to meet their families' needs. Under copyhold an individual held land from a manorial landlord in return for services. The land was originally held at the whim of the landlord but over time it was deemed to be held on terms customary to that manor. In the case of Privilege Villeinage the nature and extent of services due were ascertained; however, in the case of Pure Villeinage the individual might not know from one day to the next what service he might be called upon to perform. The service ultimately became the payment of rent.

Copyhold provides a good example of the struggle between landlord and tenant. Originally copyhold land was held at the whim of the landlord. However, tenants were gradually able to ensure that the rights were dealt with in accordance with the custom of the manor. By the early seventeenth century Sir Edward Coke was able to say:

> Now copyholders stand upon a sure ground, now they weigh not their Lord's displeasure, they shake not at every suddaine blast of winde, they eate, drinke and sleepe securely: only having a special care of the main-chance, namely, to perform carefully what duties and services so ever their tenure doth exact and custome doth require.[8]   (*The Complete Copyholder-Section* ix, 1644)

In practice the social superiority gained from granting land continued. Evidence of the feudal class structure of landowners and tenants in England can be seen still in the special church pews – sometimes boxed – that were built for the gentry to separate them from their tenants and labourers.

INDUSTRIAL SOCIETY

In the sixteenth and seventeenth centuries, feudal tenures once more began to give way to a greater emphasis on individual rights in land. In the British Isles increased urbanization and the drive to feed a growing population and its armies during a particularly turbulent period in European history meant that common land gradually disappeared.

The industrial revolution brought about the migration of people from rural communities to the fast developing towns and cities. The place of work was no longer the farm but the factory; the employer became the industrialist not the lord of the manor.

Urbanisation brought opportunities for a new generation of landlords. In 1795 T. Gisborne described the duties of a *'gentleman'* with property as the encouragement of:

> a race of honest, skilful and industrious tenants... by furnishing all of its in-habitants with constant and growing employment and thus preventing the vices and disorders which derive their origin from idleness.[9]
> (Quoted in *An Enquiry into the Duties of Men in Higher and Middle Classes of Society in Great Britain*, vol. 2, 1794; rev. 1795)

A few property owners, usually enlightened industrialists, did provide a higher standard of living and working accommodation for their employees than was the norm in Britain, in the belief that better conditions would lead to higher productivity. For example, William Lever, later Lord Leverhulme, created Port Sunlight in 1889 on the River Mersey for his soap works which he moved from Warrington. He provided commercial, industrial, residential, community and recreational buildings which were well spaced, with plenty of light and fresh air. The community buildings were paid for from a proportion of the company's profits allocated to the workers, as a form of prosperity sharing.

Sir William Lever acted out of philanthropic motives that would perhaps be less than fashionable today. Commenting on the profit scheme, he explained that he could simply have given his workers a cash bonus, but instead:

> I told them eight pounds is ... soon spent and it will not do you much good if you send it down your throats in the form of bottles of whisky, bags of sweets, or fat geese for Christmas. On the other hand, if you leave this money with me, I shall use it to provide for you everything which makes life pleasant – viz nice houses, comfortable homes, and healthy recreation. Besides, I am disposed to allow profit sharing in no other than that form.[10]
>
> (Wilson, *History of Unilever*, 1954)

All the householders worked for Lever Brothers, however, and their tenancy agreements, like their jobs, were subject to one week's notice.

Other industrialists who created model industrial villages included the Cadbury family of Quakers who built Bournville, William Hartley who created Hartley outside Liverpool for jam production and Titus Salt who built Saltaire in 1861 to house his alpaca wool business on the river Aire near Bradford.

However these enlightened examples are far outweighed by the examples of abuse, negligence and mismanagement by property owners.

A LAND FIT FOR HEROES – THE REFORMS OF THE 1920s

By the end of the nineteenth century in England and Wales, leasehold and copyhold and various divergent offshoots still existed, despite a number of attempts to simplify the land tenure system. After the First World War, a law commission established to simplify conveyancing discovered that its objective was almost impossible without first simplifying the land tenure system. It therefore made recommendations that led to the Law of Property Act 1925. Uniformity of land tenure was achieved when the Act came into effect on 1 January 1926 with copyholders becoming freeholders and the feudal system becoming extinct. No compensation for any loss occasioned to the Lord of the Manor by the abolition of copyhold tenure was received, although some recompense for any financial rights which were incidental to the copyhold, that is mining rights, was made. What did not change of course was the somewhat feudal nature of the landlord and tenant relationship.

Simplification of conveyancing was achieved as a result of the consolidation of tenure into freeholds and leaseholds under the 1925 legislation, but also by the introduction of registration of ownership under the Land Registration Act 1925. This provided for voluntary registration on transfer of ownership, although since 1990 registration has been compulsory.

Along with the reform of feudalism the twentieth century has been marked by attempts on the part of the legislature to achieve a more equable balance of power between landlords and tenants. A good example is the subject of improvements. Under the Landlord and Tenant Act 1927 the law provides that where a tenant carries out an improvement with the landlord's consent the landlord is not entitled to demand rent for the value of that improvement.

POST SECOND WORLD WAR

The move towards a more equal relationship between landlord and tenant continued after the Second World War. Under the Landlord and Tenant Act 1954, tenants were given a measure of security of tenure. This consists of the right to claim a new tenancy at an up-to-date market rent on the termination of the current tenancy, unless the landlord requires the premises for one of a specified number of reasons, including for his own use or for redevelopment.

Some of the biggest changes in the approach to property in the UK have taken place since the Second World War. During the 1950s, long term interest rates were relatively low and commercial property developers and investors could earn good returns from letting properties for 21 years or more at fixed rents. The sole intention was to secure a long term income that matched or preferably exceeded the cost of a long term mortgage. Tenants were the means by which the aim was achieved.

THE GROWTH OF THE INSTITUTIONAL INVESTOR

As inflation and interest rates increased in the mid 1960s, institutional investors began to appreciate the attraction of property. At the same time pension funds grew significantly with population growth and increasing public awareness of the need to provide for retirement. This also encouraged the growth of occupational pension schemes. Insurance companies also saw an influx of funds and until March 1984 life assurance was encouraged through the tax system with the Government paying insurance companies 15% of the gross premiums received annually.

Although most of the institutions only began seriously investing in property after the 1970s, property rapidly became a significant asset class:

By 1982, the total property assets were £16 billion for life insurance companies and £9.9 billion for pension funds. These figures represented 19.9% and 13.7% of the total assets respectively.[11]

(Mackintosh and Sykes, *A Guide to Institutional Property Investment*, 1985)

PROPERTY AS AN EQUITY INVESTMENT

Property became an equity investment and at stages of the economic cycle performed well when measured against fixed interest investments. However, as the property investor tried to maximize rents and increase the security of his investments, leases became longer and more complex and certainly less user-friendly to the tenant. For example, rent reviews were introduced initially every seven years and later every five years. In some cases, particularly during the hyper-inflation of the early 1970s and in the retail sector, reviews were introduced at three yearly intervals.

Landlords taking full advantage of their dominant position were able to insist on full repairing and insuring leases. This transferred liability for repairs and maintenance as well as for the running of buildings from expert landlords to tenants who were seldom qualified for, or interested initially in, protecting the landlords' investments. Tenants learned hard lessons as plant and machinery began to need replacement, inadequacies in the original construction came to light and liability for dilapidation increased during the lease. They slowly began to realize the full implications of the obligations and covenants that they had accepted so willingly.

At the same time, as more and more case law was established in relation to issues such as alienation clauses, inherent defects and rent reviews, lawyers tried to protect their clients' investments by creating ever more complicated clauses to reflect the judgments, the latest thinking and what was deemed to be best practice.

There seemed no limits to the efforts that landlords were prepared to make to transfer all responsibility for a building onto the tenant whose core skills were probably quite unrelated to the operation of a complex building. Indeed, professional practices flourished on the back of the adversarial nature of the landlord and tenant relationship and today many advisers in the industry who specialize in disputes have, no doubt unwittingly, a vested interest in conflict and then using the law to resolve that conflict.

It is perhaps not surprising that most tenants feel that they receive a raw deal from their landlords and this is reflected by the work of the courts. In 1994, there were 7169 proceedings in the Chancery Division of the High Court. This included 3060 related to land and 22% of those were landlord and tenant disputes. A further 36% were disputes over mortgages and charges. What a waste of human resources!

THE RISE OF THE MULTIPLE TENANT

The growth of a strong tenant lobby has been a significant factor influencing the development of property law in recent years. The current negotiating strength enjoyed by companies such as Marks and Spencer, John Lewis and Tesco often outweigh any negotiating strength held by retailers prior to the 1970s. An example would be the Landlord and Tenant Covenants Act 1995 which largely abolished the system of privity of contract under which tenants could be obliged to underwrite the performance of their assignees and pay for assignee default even many years after the tenant had parted with his lease. Legislation abolishing this system was sponsored, drafted by and steered through the Houses of Parliament by the British Retail Consortium.

CURRENT ATTITUDES

Part of the problem is that the property sector has traditionally regarded the large investor as its customer. Rarely have the occupying organization or the people who use the building every day been considered as customers. This has meant that property companies have had good reason to concentrate on maximizing their returns by signing long-term deals that provide investors with the long-term security of income they demand.

The complex structure of legal documents for property transactions has as its essence the protection of those who own, transfer and grant rights and the long term security of their financial positions. For reasons of history and custom, these parties have been dominant and documents have in the main been one-sided, although statutes in England such as the Landlord and Tenant Act 1954 protected, and in some instances enhanced, tenants' rights.

Yet terminology and structures support the traditional approach, with great reliance on the law to settle confrontations between landlords seeking to enforce their rights and tenants attempting to escape their obligations.

Landlord or lessor are terms that imply not merely possession but also a relationship with an inferior, that is a tenant or lessee. And seen from the perspective of most other industries, they are quaint terms that have their roots in the feudal system. They certainly do not imply a relationship between two equal parties nor between a supplier and a consumer of products or services.

Reliance on the historic terms, such as landlord and tenant, lessor and lessee and on a vast array of statutory and case law, does little to advance the concept of customer service and is one of the hurdles to moving owners towards a more customer focused approach.

'Rack rent' is perhaps the term that most strongly evokes feudal times. It is a curiosity that is still in use today to describe open market rent. The term evokes images of the medieval torture chamber being used as a means of extracting the highest rent!

"AGREEING THE RACK RENT"

What a difference from the terminology of an American shopping catalogue:

> A customer is the most important visitor on our premises. He is not dependent on us – we are dependent on him. He is not an outsider in our business – he is part of it. We are not doing him a favour by serving him – he is doing us a favour by giving us the opportunity to do so.[12]
>
> (Successories, Summer 1994 Catalogue, p. 2)

The next chapter considers the driving forces for adopting an approach to property management that leaves the residue of the feudal system behind and focuses on tenants as valued customers.

Notes

1. Cheshire, G.C. and Burn, E.H. (1994) *Modern Law of Real Property*, 15th edn (London: Butterworths).
2. Brodrick, G. (1881) *English Land and English Landlords* (London: Cassell & Co. Reprinted in 1968 by Gregg International Publishers, Farnborough, Hampshire)
3. Salway, P. (1981) *Roman Britain* (Oxford: Oxford University Press).
4. Finberg, H.P.R. (ed.) (1972) *Agrarian History of England and Wales*, Vol. 1 (Cambridge: Cambridge University Press).
5. Kiralfy, A.K. (1962) *Potter's Historical Introduction to English Law and its Institutions*, 4th edn (London: Sweet & Maxwell).
6. Maitland, F.W. (1897) *Domesday Book and Beyond* (Cambridge: Cambridge University Press).
7. Stubbs, W.S. (1866) *Constitutional History of England* (Oxford: Clarendon Press).
8. Coke, Sir E. (1644) *The Compleate Copyholder – Section IX* (London: Matthew Walbanck and Richard Best).
9. Gisborne, T. (1794) Quoted in, *An Enquiry into the Duties of Men in Higher and Middle Classes of Society in Great Britain*, Vol. 2, p. 385 (first published in London 1794, revised in 1795, and re-published in London that year in two volumes: now out of print).
10. Wilson, C. (1954) *History of Unilever* (London: Cassell).
11. Mackintosh, A. and S. Sykes (1985) *A Guide to Institutional Property Investment* (London: Macmillan).
12. Successories, Inc., Illinois, USA (Summer 1994 Catalogue, p. 23). Used with permission and published by Successories, Inc., all rights reserved.

2 Drivers for Change

Chapter 1 outlined the characteristics of the property business and the evolution of the traditional approach to property management. This chapter considers the forces upon occupiers of property and, as a consequence, how owners must manage their portfolios to achieve competitive advantage. The traditional transaction focus of property owners is contrasted with the relationship focus that has been adopted widely by service industries in response to customer needs. A relationship focus is fundamental to the approach that this book recommends.

Focusing on the customer is so contrary to the traditions of property that the intuitive rationale of building relationships may need quantitative proof. Therefore the chapter ends with a simple example of how fundamental change leads to improved profitability and indicates how some property owners are already adopting this approach.

Why change? Quite simply, the customer for property has changed, its suppliers and markets have changed, and its aspirations and goals have changed. Suppliers of business property are no different from any other supplier of goods or services; they must react positively to their tenants' changing requirements, as their competitors will. Simply because things have been the same for a very long time in the UK property market does not mean that change is not happening now, or that change is just a short-term reaction to a cyclical market imbalance. Just look at some of the many forces at play in business today.

GLOBALIZATION

The world is simply a far more competitive place in which to do business. The drive for business success has led to global expansion to capture new and developing markets and diversify activities. Increasingly, property owners are dealing with occupiers that are either managed internationally or have suppliers or markets overseas. Much of this expansion of activity is in response to increased mobility created by advances in telecommunications and information technology (IT), falling trade barriers and converging consumer tastes.

13

The world is becoming smaller with fewer, larger organizations that have an increasing impact on people's lives. Many businesses may appear to be domestic but in reality are small parts of international groups. Think of car manufacturers or insurance companies for example. Today, firms anywhere in the world can reach any market. They can bring to bear the power of new technologies, low-paid and highly-skilled workers, and large amounts of capital.

Many of the consequences of globalization have happened almost unnoticed. Who would have thought a decade ago that you might ring a freephone number in London to speak to a telephone operative in Ireland to buy a personal computer, containing components from the Far East, shipped from the USA, without leaving the comfort of your armchair? Think how things might be 10 years from now.

COMPETITION

Slow economic growth in advanced economies and the opening up of markets has heightened the impact of global competition. This has led to pressure on margins and on profitability. The recession of the 1990s put a significant squeeze on company profits. Reduced profits and in many cases significant losses restricted the ability of companies to grow. In 1990 and 1991, in the depths of recession, over 20% of the Fortune 500 corporations posted losses. General Motors, Ford and IBM between them lost about $15 billion (*Fortune*, 20 April 1992).[1] Although the recession in Europe may not have been so severe, it lasted an unexpectedly long time.

Pressure on margins forced companies to look more closely at their overheads, including their requirements for space. The resulting cutbacks in the space occupied contributed to the collapse of property companies in the first half of the 1990s. Many occupiers are emerging from survival mode, but they keep a close watch on whether the various parts of their operations are contributing to shareholder value, are expendable or should be out-sourced from external suppliers.

CORPORATE DOWNSIZING

New ways of working and rapid advances in IT have enabled organizations of all varieties to reduce staff levels and the property overheads that they carry. In some businesses, senior management sets targets for staff numbers and space costs, and property disposals follow.

For example, British Telecommunications plc (BT) launched a huge cost-saving programme after its privatization. This involved the elimination of many thousands of jobs, as well as a review of its real estate which is its third largest cost. BT set real estate targets to cut total occupancy costs and space from £1.2 billion per annum in 1991 to £750 million per annum by 1999. Despite the magnitude of the task, the company is well on its way to meeting its goals. Similarly, Dunn & Bradstreet launched an initiative in 1993 to reduce the space it used by 30%, and to cut occupancy costs by 25%, or from 7% to 4.2% of revenue (Mahlon Apgar IV, *Harvard Business Review*, 1995).[2]

Other organizations have used mergers and acquisitions as a spring-board for.downsizing. For example, Chemical Bank's merger with Manufacturers Hanover in 1991 led to two years of consolidation in the UK; net space fell from 70 000 m² to 30 000 m², its 11 buildings became three and occupancy costs fell by more than half (J.B. Edwards, 1996).[3] Five years later a similar consolidation is taking place following the merger of the new Chemical Bank with The Chase Manhattan Bank.

Many businesses have woken up to the true impact of property over-heads on profitability. Although recession has reduced their revenues, many businesses are tied into excessive property costs as a consequence of the 1980s boom in rents, and maintenance and insurance costs and local taxes continue to rise with inflation. The percentage of revenue eaten up by occupancy cost, 'the affordability ratio', sets the limit that companies are prepared to pay for real estate and facilities. It can act as a key driver in management decision-making in forward-thinking organizations.

By way of illustration, take IBM which saw its worldwide revenues grow 8% per annum compound between 1982 and 1992, whilst occupancy costs grew by 15% per annum. Its affordability ratio therefore doubled from 1.5% to over 3%. Although that may still seem low, if IBM had suc-ceeded in keeping the ratio constant it would have cut its occupancy cost by $1 billion in 1992; almost half of the loss it reported that year (J.B. Edwards, 1996).[4] The UK would show up similar examples, were it not for less-stringent company reporting regulations that do not require occupancy costs to be shown in the same way.

NEW TECHNOLOGY

New technology is changing the way people work within and communi-cate between workplaces. It is also changing fundamentally how properties perform. Those buildings that cannot meet the needs of modern IT and telecommunications are destined to perform badly as investments as well as for their occupiers. Occupiers above all require flexible space that meets the changing needs of project-driven work-groups. Companies must be able to adapt space to their technologies, not to adapt the technologies to the limitations of their space.

More and more businesses are communicating internally and externally via electronic mail, and the impact of video technology will no doubt soon begin to be felt more widely. Businesses need less space for paper storage and are encouraging greater freedom of movement through the use of cordless technology. It may not be long before the arrival of the first wireless and paperless office? Yet businesses are trying to ensure that they do not have peopleless offices, by increasing the intensity of usage in terms of more people per m² and more hours of occupancy. Technology plays an important part in achieving these objectives.

In many large companies and in much of the public sector, technology has replaced whole layers of administration. For example, triggered by recession and competition but enabled by technology, the numbers employed in banking have fallen significantly; in the leading British banks by 15% between 1989 and 1993 alone (*The Milliken Report*, 1996).[5]

Technological change is not of course limited to the office. New manufacturing techniques and logistics operations are changing the use of industrial and warehouse space. In retailing, the widespread use of electronic point-of-sale inventory control, and the emergence of home shopping have all had an impact on retailers' choice of space and its location.

Technology is also changing where people work as well as how they work. It may seem strange that a call to directory enquiries in London for a local telephone number is answered in Scotland, but technology makes normal geographic boundaries irrelevant. It also allows flexibility in organizations. By splitting front and back office tasks businesses have been able to locate offices where it suits their staff without their customers being affected, and more people can work from home. For example, a quarter of the 4000 UK employees of the computer company Digital Equipment Corporation have flexible work patterns rather than traditional office arrangements, saving £3.5 million a year (R. Donkin, *Financial Times*, 1995).[6]

Change will continue, as a result of increasing access to new technology, in ways that are impossible to predict. For example, the impact of the Internet is only just beginning to become clear, although one estimate is that more than 40 million people are connected to it (J. Bird, *Management Today*, 1996).[7] Not so long ago the Internet was solely a means of communication for academic bodies and the military.

WORLD-CLASS EXPECTATIONS

This fifth business driver is perhaps the most challenging of all for property owners. All customers have become more demanding consumers and expect better standards of service, quality and value for money to persuade them to part with hard-earned money. Individuals and corporations are far more discriminating in their buying decisions and through world travel and the media have an international awareness and expectation of performance. They operate on a world stage and have every reason to expect their landlords to meet world-class rather than local standards. It is simply no longer sufficient to say 'This is how we do it in this country'.

Landlords must also appreciate that their tenant customers will be making business decisions in a global context. An occupier in the UK might not relocate within the country at all, but move somewhere with a more appropriate basis of occupation.

Suppliers of space must take on board occupiers' concerns with the well-being of their stakeholders. This necessitates greater understanding through communication and flexibility to ensure that occupiers' standards are met, not the preconceived standards of the landlord. Occupiers also want to project the right image, both externally with customers and suppliers, and internally with their labour force. And occupiers' growing concerns for their local environment and communities will also have to be accommodated.

THE RESULT IS CHANGE

The writing is on the wall. Globalization, competition, corporate downsizing, new technology and world-class expectations are all threats to the status quo. The market has changed; occupiers are striving to retain flexibility in all they do and they are more and more conscious of the impact of property on their businesses. Where does this leave the property sector?

Although many surveying practices undertake research on vacancy rates, take-up rates of new and second-hand space, rents and investment yield trends, little or no research is undertaken into how landlords are satisfying the increasingly demanding requirements of tenants and prospective tenants. What is clear is that the drivers for change will continue to make ever more challenging demands on landlords. Even today we know that something like 10% of office space in the UK is vacant, that a trip down almost any high street will provide evidence of empty shops. Institutional owners have seen the value of their property portfolios drop, fuelled by the rise in vacancy rates. The trend has brought some property companies to their knees.

One outcome of these trends is the demise of the 25-year institutional lease, except perhaps for the most specialist buildings. Lease lengths have fallen significantly since the peak of the 1980s boom. Research by Drivers Jonas shows that in 1993 the average retail lease was for 11 years compared with 22 years in 1989 (Malcolm Hull, partner in Drivers Jonas Limited, 1995).[8] This trend is not expected to go into reverse when economic activity picks up, and a number of major occupiers have voiced their intentions publicly in this regard (*News Analysis, CSW*, 1993).[9]

Clearly, landlords will no longer be able to sit back and take a passive role in property management. They can no longer rely on producing a building for letting on a long occupational lease and enjoying the benefits of rental growth and capital appreciation as of right. They must understand their markets and listen to their customers. They must build relationships with occupiers, not just sign them up and enforce the terms of the lease. In short they must behave much the same way as other businesses and grasp with both hands the concept of customer service and the opportunities that it presents.

There is a wealth of literature on satisfying customers. Examples of initiatives from leaders in a variety of industries show how to develop a customer focus and outline the rewards to be reaped. These companies' actions are in response to many of the same drivers that affect property. There is something very deep-rooted in their commitment, and their motivation is derived from the well-established principles of customer service, choice and value for money that have been the corner-stones of retailing and most other industries for as long as anyone can remember; but property is different.

There is rarely any doubt who the customer is when someone walks into a shop, arranges insurance by telephone or hires a car. Yet ask a property manager who the customer is and the most likely answer will be the landlord. It is akin to expecting retailers to name their shareholders as their customers.

Of course, a company selling something or offering a service usually sees or speaks to its customer on a daily basis and so quickly appreciates that a satisfied customer will return. In property management, contact between the customer and the supplier is infrequent and this may be one reason why the link between customer service and property performance has not been identified.

CUSTOMER FOCUS IN PROPERTY MANAGEMENT

The concept of serving the customer seems far removed from the statutory framework of landlord and tenant legislation, with its language of protection and rights. Customer service is about responding to the customer's right to choose in a positive way. No supplier has the right to continued custom, and winning and retaining a customer becomes the foremost objective of customer focused property management.

To meet this objective, property management must be approached with an understanding of what management means from the customer's perspective. There is a need to recognize and reconcile the traditional conflicts between owner and occupier and to appreciate that there is a different way of doing things. Management must be viewed in the context of the property supply chain, which starts with identifying a market and flows through design and construction to delivery and occupation. Property management does not sit in isolation from other property activities.

Knowing the business

The keys to an effective customer focus in any business are to know what is driving change, to identify the objectives of the business and of customers, and to appreciate what is valued by customers and what distinguishes the business from its competitors.

How do customers' objectives compare with property owners'? In Table 2.1, the main objectives of the parties can be clearly seen to be at odds with each other. The reason is simply that owners want income from their investment properties and set about securing that income and maintaining the value of the investment, while occupiers see property as a facility in which to carry out their activities. The value that occupiers attribute to the facility is not measured in terms of rent or yield but in terms of how it contributes to their business, by revenue or profit. These objectives are, on the face of it, incompatible, but owners will not achieve their goals unless they meet the needs of occupiers. Owners that are flexible, innovative and determined will find ways to reconcile these conflicting objectives. Owners that can respond successfully to the challenge will outlive their competitors.

Table 2.1   Property conflicts

Owner objectives	*Occupier objectives*
Property viewed as income-producing asset	Property viewed as facility
Maximize income	Minimize occupancy costs
Certainty of income	Certainty of occupation
Privity of contract	No contingent liabilities
Minimize expenditure	Minimize expenditure
Avoid vacancies	Flexible term
Maximize asset value	Productive environment for staff, processes and customers
Risk avoidance	Risk avoidance
Asset enhancement through development when appropriate	Security of occupation
Low management responsibility	Avoidance of non-core activities
Management of conflict	Avoidance of conflict
Asset liquidity	Flexible disposal options
Management as an asset	Management for the business

Knowing the product and service

A customer focused strategy is about differentiating a business from its competitors and adding value for occupiers by management action. To know the product or service is to understand the benefits for customers. The important notion to appreciate is that property management is not about the property business, but about the accommodation or space business. The core product is space, not bricks and mortar. Once this is understood a property company is well on the way to seeing what occupiers want, and how it can earn rewards in the long run by meeting their needs.

Of course, providing space is not enough. Property managers must add value to this core product through what marketeers call the 'product surround' or 'augmented product'. Figure 2.1 identifies some of the main areas in which customer value can be added, and these areas of opportunity are covered throughout this book.

Retaining tenants

A property company can take a further step towards redirecting itself by thinking about how management activities fit with the whole property

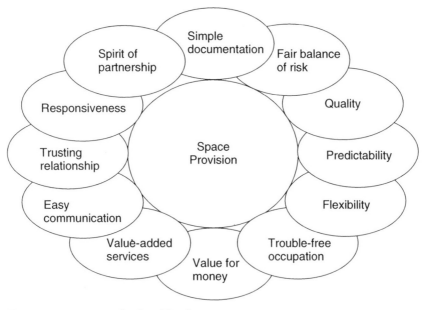

Figure 2.1   Areas which add value

supply process, and to split the process into pre-transaction, transaction and post-transaction phases. It then becomes clear how it can achieve real benefits by focusing on the occupier as a customer it wants to retain. One way of illustrating this is to overlay the three phases on to a marketeer's representation of customer service, the ladder of loyalty, or what might be renamed in a property context the ladder of retention (Figure 2.2).

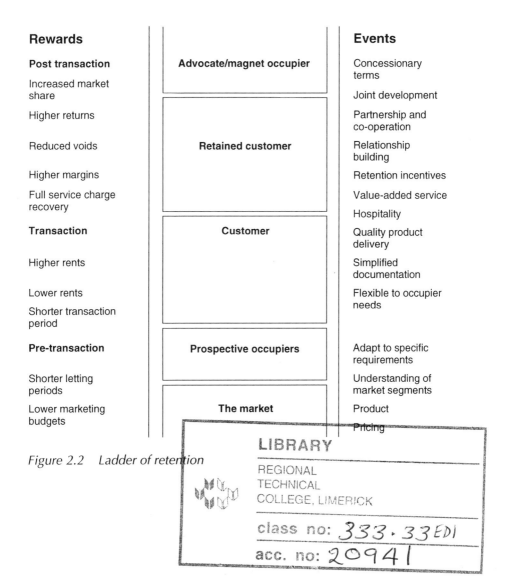

Figure 2.2   Ladder of retention

Retaining tenants is a lot easier and less expensive than finding new ones, and becomes a fundamental goal of property management. It requires a concerted effort to provide occupiers with the level of service they would expect from their other suppliers, and the same level of service that their customers would expect from them.

The ladder shows that focusing on occupier need right from the start helps identify the likely occupier for a building. Giving the prospective occupier the confidence that the property will be managed well, simplifying the transaction process and being responsive to the occupier's needs are likely to secure the occupier and earn more rent. Reinforcing the occupier's selection decision after the transaction by being hospitable and responsive encourages development of a productive long-term relationship, which will avoid significant re-letting costs and ultimately lead to higher returns. With consumer goods or most forms of service, an especially-pleased customer will recommend the supplier to others and there seems no reason why this should not apply to property.

Owners of large property portfolios that can offer a variety of locations are in a particularly good position to develop a brand and to benefit from customer brand loyalty. It is feasible that an occupier will grow with a landlord and follow that owner as well as acting as a draw for others.

"TENANT RETENTION"

The question can be put: why retain tenants on short leases when longer leases would lock tenants into contracts from which there is no escape? For specialist buildings there will continue to be good reason for the landlord to secure longer-term security of income, but for this to be the norm would be to maintain the conflicts of the past to try to create a successful future. Even if market conditions reversed the trend towards shorter leases, passive management in the traditional style will not secure the levels of return that investors from property can expect from treating occupiers as customers.

Take the example of business centres providing furnished offices as a model for what can be achieved by adding value to short-term occupation. Space provision is treated as a business, not as an investment asset – high returns on the basic space through flexible leasing are augmented by returns from add-on office services and facilities such as reception staff, office equipment and catering. Managers of commercial property portfolios would do well to benchmark their performance against the serviced office sector to achieve best practice.

Building relationships

The business centre example further illustrates how forging relationships adds to the rewards of active management. Table 2.2 helps to distinguish the relationship-driven organization from the deal-driven organization and acts as a reminder of how a business can direct its efforts to satisfying its customers.

Table 2.2   Relationship-driven and deal-driven organizations

Transaction marketing	Relationship marketing
Focus on the deal	Focus on customer retention
Focus on property features	Focus on property benefits
Short time-scale	Long time-scale
Emphasis on asset value	Emphasis on cash flow
Limited occupier commitment	High occupier commitment
Avoidance of occupier contact	Communication with occupier encouraged
Emphasis on quality of the building for investment needs	Emphasis on functionality of the building for occupier's business needs
Shareholder/investor as customer	Occupier as customer
Inflexible leasing	Flexible leasing
Win–lose mentality	Win–win mentality
Tenant pays for all	Tenant receives fair value

It is easy to imagine the outcome of a customer survey about the perception of different business sectors; landlords would be among the least popular. For this reason alone it is important that long-term commitment is required to build a new business relationship that in the early days the tenant will view with scepticism.

There is no short-term fix, just a long road that in the end will deliver the benefits of satisfied customers.

THE REWARDS

It would be easy to interpret this new approach to property management as one that passes value to the tenant at the expense of the landlord. In the short term, during a period of adjustment, this may be the case, but is it a price worth paying?

How in the longer term does satisfaction convert into rewards for the property owner, and how might those rewards be measured?

Reduced marketing periods

Accurate identification of the market enhances letting prospects. Similarly, building a reputation for good management and establishing a brand that has the trust of the market gives an edge on competitors. Management efficiency can and should be demonstrated in tangible ways, with tenant survey information made available to prospective occupiers. The better the story, the longer the stay, the shorter the void!

Lower marketing costs

Reducing the time on the market significantly reduces outgoings. Fees and marketing expenses will be less, service charge income will be greater and the owner will have a smaller rates bill. These have a serious impact on cash flow.

Shorter transaction periods

If a company knows its property and its customers' needs it can prepare documentation over which there should be little disagreement. Simplifying and standardizing the process saves time and money.

Lower fees

Avoiding disputes with tenants and settling rent reviews amicably saves management time and professional fees, as well as encouraging tenant loyalty.

Improved service charge recovery

Providing tenants with what they want and not just with what an owner thinks they want, as well as involving tenants in decision making, is likely to result in better and faster recovery of service costs.

Facilities management

There is also scope for improved margins through extending service provision, particularly in facilities management where there are enormous opportunities for providing services so that occupiers can concentrate on their core activities.

New products

A landlord is in an ideal position to sell new products and services to a tenant that, unlike most consumers, stays in one place sometimes for years on end.

A comparison with other businesses may give a glimpse of the future. At EuroDisney the property could be regarded as the hotels, but they are simply there to secure customers who spend money on the attractions. The attractions and the retailing make the real money, not the hotels. In Las Vegas, the hotels also support the profit making from gambling, shows, food and drink.

Is BAA plc in the aviation business? Owning airports such as Heathrow and Gatwick would indicate that it is! On the other hand, the company has over the last few years moved from a position where almost all its revenue was from airline charges to one where almost 50% is from retail income. Perhaps in the future, some creative landlords will see rent as almost a loss-leader with the real money being made from value-added services and products!

Higher rents

Better value for money services translate into a better value for money building compared with the competition. This in turn provides an opportunity for premium rents, either on letting, rent review or renewal.

Reduced voids

Holding on to occupiers on renewal or avoiding occupiers exercising their mid-term break options means continued positive cash flow rather than unnecessary outgoings. Every situation needs to be judged on its merits, but inducing occupiers to stay will almost always be a top priority. Although some occupiers' reasons for moving, such as changes in markets or corporate restructuring, may be beyond the influence of even the best landlord or property manager, owners can do much to reduce tenant defections through good management. The ability to retain tenants will be a key skill of tomorrow's property manager.

MEASURING SUCCESS

To really appreciate how it pays to serve the customer you need to measure the impact. This is likely in future to be a subject of much research. Studies have already been undertaken in the USA into defection rates, to quantify the impact on profit of keeping customers and to learn from customers that do leave. One American study compares office building management with other businesses such as credit cards and insurance brokerage (Reichheld and Sasser, *Harvard Business Review*, 1990).[10] The research found that reducing defections by just 5% led to a 40% increase in the net present value of the profit stream expected during the occupancy of an office building by an average customer. In other words, there was a positively-geared relationship between keeping tenants and future profits; a small reduction in defections meant much larger profits.

Take a very simplified example. Suppose offices are let at £200 per m^2. What is the net impact on cash flow of not securing a renewal on the same terms?

As well as lost annual income while the property is unlet, there are the following costs per m^2: service charge £50, empty rates £60, agents' fees £20, marketing and legal fees £20. The net result is a change from +£200 to –£150, a cash flow loss of £350.

Translating this into a portfolio context, assume 10 identical properties, two of which are vacant through defections:

Income	8 × £200 =	£1600
Outgoings	2 × £150 =	£ 300
Net income		£1300

Now prevent one defection, that is a change in defections from 20% to 10%:

Income	9 × £200 =	£1800
Outgoings	1 × £150 =	£ 150
Net income		£1650

Thus a 10% improvement in defections produces a 27% improvement in cash flow. If we look at the effect in capital value terms of reducing the vacancy rate the additional geared effect on value of the yield should not be ignored, nor should the discount rate differential between a fully-let portfolio and a poorly managed and occupied portfolio.

These examples are only a simple illustration. But they show that good management will be reflected in improved cash flow and capital value.

CONCLUSION

Putting the occupier first is a big step forward in the property business, but there are signs of a turnaround in attitudes. Landlords are beginning to organize themselves with the occupier in mind, for example by dividing the management of their portfolios by use rather than by location. The large quoted property companies are even voicing their concern for the customer in their financial reports. The occupier also has the support of the government which launched a study in May 1993 of the workings of the commercial property market, culminating in the publication in December 1995 of a document called *Commercial Property Leases in England & Wales: Code of Practice*.[11]

This chapter promotes the good sense of establishing a closer link and a less adversarial relationship between landlord and tenant. But more than that, it is about meeting the objectives of ownership through meeting the objectives of occupation. The rationale is simple and the rewards many. The following chapters are about implementing the strategy.

Notes

1. 'The Fortune 500. It was the worst of years' (*Fortune*, 20 April 1992).
2. Mahlon Apgar IV (1995) 'Managing Real Estate to Build Value', *Harvard Business Review*, November–December, pp. 162–79.
3. Edwards, J.B. (1996) 'Satisfied Customers'. Presentation to British Property Federation, 1 February.
4. Ibid.
5. *The Milliken Report: Space Futures* (The Henley Centre, March 1996, p. 6).

6.   Donkin, R. (1995) 'Tales of the Office Nomad', *The Financial Times Limited*, 29 May.
7.   Bird, J. (1996) 'Untangling the Web', *Management Today*, March.
8.   'Commercial Leases: The Structural Revolution' (Malcolm Hull, MA, ARICS, Partner Drivers Jonas Limited May, 1995).
9.   '25-Year Lease: Breaking the Landlord's Hold' (*News Analysis*, CSW – The Property Week, 10 June 1993).
10. Reichheld, F.F. and W.E. Sasser Jnr (1990) 'Zero Defection: Quality Comes to Services', *Harvard Business Review*, September–October, pp. 105–11.
11. Royal Institute of Chartered Surveyors Business Services (1995) *Commercial Property Leases in England & Wales: Code of Practice* (London: RICS). Reproduced with the permission of the Commercial Leases Group which owns the copyright.

3 Building Blocks to Customer Service

The previous chapter considered the worldwide trends that are encouraging property owners to adopt a customer friendly approach. This chapter looks at how to create a customer focused business. In other words how does a property company turn the concept of customer service into reality?

Some lessons about how to set up or reshape a property business to focus on the customer can be learned from leading property owners in the USA. Nonetheless, BAA plc discovered from its research that there was no standard model for the property industry. However, much has been written on the process of managing change and a number of models of best practice can be found in other industries.

BAA plc first had to research and then create its own model, called the Property Challenge. This is based on the experience of managing change in other industries and in other parts of BAA plc. The model focuses on the key steps that any property business needs to address to make the journey from traditional to customer focused property management.

This chapter outlines the model and its six Building Blocks, and the blocks are explained in detail in subsequent chapters. The model will not result in an instant cure but it provides a simple commonsense framework around which real customer focus can be achieved, leading in the longer term to a more sustainable business.

THE PROPERTY CHALLENGE MODEL

- Building Block 1   Defining the customer
- Building Block 2   Researching what the customer wants
- Building Block 3   Creating a mission for the organization
- Building Block 4   Leadership, empowerment, training and communication
- Building Block 5   Process improvement and information management
- Building Block 6   Measuring success and benchmarking

BLOCK 1   DEFINING THE CUSTOMER

It may seem an obvious point to make but a company wishing to adopt a customer focused approach first needs to understand who the customer is. Equally important is the need to define each customer group within the current or potential customer base. The reason is simple – different customer groups have different needs. Who are a property owner's customers?

Traditionally, as shown in Chapter 1, the property sector has seen its main customer as the investing owner, usually a major insurance company or pension fund, rather than the corporate occupier or actual user of the accommodation. The prime focus therefore has been on maximizing financial returns through the creation of trouble-free long-term income streams. Investing owners are important stakeholders in any property venture but to a manager of property they are not customers.

Customers are the companies and individuals who occupy buildings. A truly customer focused business must focus on both customer groups and must not lose sight of their different needs. The logic is simple; dissatisfied staff will complain to the senior managers who make buying decisions about property. The perception of a property decision-maker about a building or landlord is likely to be shaped as much by the number of complaints they receive from individual occupiers as by the rent level or overall building quality. This perception will be critical when the time comes to decide whether to renew a lease or expand into new space owned by an existing landlord. So the customer is as much the individual as the corporate tenant.

BLOCK 2   RESEARCHING WHAT THE CUSTOMER WANTS

Having defined the customers, the next step is to find out what they want and then measure their satisfaction against the service currently being provided.

The key to refocusing a business is to 'listen, listen and listen' and then take action. Regular surveys that become the ears of the organization must be undertaken. Customer satisfaction surveys have become commonplace in many industries and yet they are relatively rare in the property sector. In itself this reflects the property world's lack of customer focus. As Sir John Egan, Chief Executive, BAA plc has commented:

> Measurement is one of the key elements to a customer focused business – if you can't measure it, you can't improve it.[1]

The purpose of a survey is to identify what customers or a representative sample of them consider to be the strong and weak areas of a company's service delivery. The information gathered can be used to focus management attention on what are the key issues from the tenant's perspective. Without this information a property manager is in effect running blind and could be in danger of misdirecting effort to actions that are of no relevance to the tenant.

There are two principal types of survey; quantitative and qualitative. In a quantitative survey the customer gives marks in response to a list of questions, usually on a scale of 1 to 5, or 1 to 10. An example is BAA's tenant survey carried out face to face with 200 customers each year by an independent survey team. The survey has been running long enough to show clear trends that give confidence about the accuracy of the survey. Depending on the circumstances, surveys can also be carried out on the telephone or by postal questionnaire.

In a qualitative survey an individual or group of customers will be interviewed, usually by an independent company employed by the property owner. The comments will not be representative necessarily of the group as a whole but nevertheless will give invaluable information. These focus groups can be drawn from a particular building or sample of buildings and where appropriate concentrate on particular issues that the landlord feels are in need of improved performance.

These survey techniques are not sufficient in their own right and should be used to supplement traditional forms of feedback such as meetings with customers, correspondence and telephone calls. No chance should be missed to gather information on the question: how are we doing?

Like all good things, customer satisfaction measures can be used and abused. Professor Ranko Bon commented:

> Beware of bugging your customers with silly questionnaires. It's better to spend time making your customers happy than to know how happy your customers are.[2]
> (Professor Ranko Bon, University of Reading, 1996)

Owners should avoid making excessive demands on their customers' time, and wherever possible should use 'unobtrusive measures' of satisfaction, such as the number and frequency of calls to a help desk. Bon says that it is better to measure a few indicators often than to measure many infrequently.

The ability to find out what customers want is fast becoming a science but the starting point is a wish to know. If that wish is there, then the rest should be easy; an ability to question openly, to listen carefully and respond positively with action.

BLOCK 3   CREATING A MISSION FOR THE ORGANIZATION

This stage is in many ways the most critical. It comes when the desire of an individual to focus on the customer and improve performance is communicated to all those involved in delivering service. This would include senior management colleagues, front-line staff and suppliers; in fact, everyone who can have an impact on the customer.

It is often, but not always, the leader of an organization who initiates the drive to become customer focused. Nonetheless it is always the case that change cannot occur without visible leadership support from the top. This is the first step along a long road, and the challenge of creating a common mission or commitment to focusing a business on meeting the needs of its customers should not be underestimated. Attitudes developed over many years do not change overnight and changing company culture takes time and resources. This is even more the case in a sector such as property, where attitudes are entrenched and legitimized to a substantial degree, certainly in England, by the statutory framework of landlord and tenant legislation.

A company's mission may be set down within a formally-published mission statement. Mission statements have proliferated in recent years and can be found prominently displayed in a wide range of businesses. One might imagine that the simple posting of a mission statement has some magical power to bring about change – but of course it does not. Mission statements have become in some companies more of a virility symbol than a genuine communication tool.

A mission statement or set of values has no real benefit unless it is communicated effectively to every corner of an organization and its contents are fully understood and believed in. Even more, all staff need the resources to deliver the aims embodied within the mission statement. The real value of a mission statement is that it provides clear direction and focus and allows everyone to share the values and goals of an organization. The key, however, remains for the mission to be converted to realizable objectives and for performance to be monitored routinely.

The mission statement for the Chicago property managers LaSalle is typical:

> Each property will apply our management and marketing systems to become recognized by its tenants for providing the highest level of quality tenant service available in its market.[3] (LaSalle Partners Management Limited, 1992)

The key words are:

- *systems* – demanding the use of a defined standardized process for property management and marketing;
- *recognized by its tenants* – focusing on the tenant as customer, not the building owner;
- *highest* – setting the target at the equivalent of world best;
- *service* – defining the service relationship;
- *available in its market* – emphasising the competitive environment in which the business operates.

Mission statements should also target achievable and therefore believable goals. A mission to fly to the moon for Christmas will hardly gain much support! In line with the ability to deliver, a mission should not be cast in stone but able to evolve over time. The first step might be 'focusing on customers' needs' and when that has been achieved 'meeting customers' expectations'. Perhaps one day a property management organization might even be able to deliver and therefore believe in a statement that requires the organization to 'exceed the expectations of customers'. A mission statement can either be a motivating rallying call or a collection of words that generate nothing but scepticism.

BLOCK 4   LEADERSHIP, EMPOWERMENT, TRAINING AND COMMUNICATION

The real commitment and energy of a leader is essential if an organization is to change its culture which, after all, may have developed over generations.

> You are an architect of the corporate culture. You shape it by how you behave. Every single thing you do serves as one more building block in the habit patterns that make up the personality, the culture, the company. In time the culture takes on a life of its own. It gains power and influence. And as the habits grow stronger, the culture begins to shape your behaviour more and more. Culture can be very controlling. But powerful as it might be, the culture cannot change without permission from the people. The problems come when the world changes but the culture can't...because people in the organization won't give it a chance. Today, in our world of high-velocity change, the culture needs your help in order to break its bad habits. You need to teach it better ways to behave. It relies on you to give it a new set of responses that hold more promise for the future.[4]
> (Pritchett, *Culture Shift*, 1996)

Delivering even good levels of customer service requires the full commitment of the leader and of every member of staff within a business; there should be no weak links. It follows, therefore, that the achievement of improved performance requires the direct contribution of staff at all levels and at all locations. This will make particularly strong demands on front-line staff who may have been limited traditionally in their ability to respond to customer needs without seeking higher-level approval.

But customer service requires that fast and effective solutions are provided for customers, and therefore all staff need to be able to respond positively to meet customer requirements. This means a relaxation of traditional controls that hamper the delivery of service, a process that is often known as empowerment.

Red tape can come in many forms. Areas to look at include financial and other signing powers, procedures for ordering goods and services, complaints and approvals procedures and so on. Often procedures put in place to control cost or reduce the risk of misuse of company resources work against the genuine needs of customers.

However, empowerment does not mean giving *carte blanche* to all staff to do exactly what they want. The key to empowerment is to define boundaries and encourage staff to go up to those boundaries but not beyond. BAA has adopted the idea of green, amber and red zones with different levels of responsibility to help define boundaries. New areas of responsibility may well be greater than previously and staff will need to be positively encouraged, and trained, to expand their activities. In this way they will enjoy the experience of greater responsibility which brings with it greater responsiveness to the customers.

In many organizations, fear of failure and the resulting blame may deter a member of staff from extending their responsibilities. Staff may also be held back from achieving their full potential by ineffective training, poor information systems, or a lack of good internal communication.

BLOCK 5   PROCESS IMPROVEMENT AND INFORMATION MANAGEMENT

At this point a property company knows its customers, understands their requirements, has a mission to deliver what the customers want and has a motivated and customer focused team ready to act. But how can improvements in quality, service and cost be delivered? The answer is through excellent processes supported by quality management information.

This Building Block is in many ways the toughest of all and first involves an understanding of the processes that make up a business. There are a number of definitions of a business process. Hammer and Champy (*Re-engineering the Corporation*, 1993) define it as a collection of activities that takes one or more kinds of input and creates an output that is of value to the customer.[5]

In simple terms, a business process is a series of steps. By examining each step it is possible to identify non-productive tasks which may delay or add expense to the delivery of the service or product to the customer. By removing these steps, the process can be improved and efficiencies realized. Process improvement is aimed at improving quality and service while at the same time reducing cost. This apparent contradiction is the key to running a quality company. The combination of skilled staff and efficient business processes is the hallmark of a customer focused organization.

However, the key processes that make up each business are often not understood within the business. A complication is that it is not uncommon for processes to cross departmental or functional boundaries and also for processes to involve outside suppliers and agencies.

Traditionally, many managers shy away from crossing boundaries and seeking improvements to the process as a whole, preferring to stick to their areas of immediate responsibility. This often leads to the customer receiving less than optimal service or product quality.

BLOCK 6   MEASURING SUCCESS AND BENCHMARKING

How does a company know if it is making progress? The data obtained from customer surveys will be valuable in itself for identifying priority areas for action. However, measurement is also an invaluable tool for comparing performance within a portfolio or between portfolios in different ownership. This allows the property manager to identify the best performance and compare their performance against this standard. This comparison or benchmarking is a key element in setting targets to raise performance.

Benchmarking also enables customers to compare service delivery with the best experience they have received in any industry worldwide. For example, a customer may compare the speed of replacing a defective light-bulb in their hotel room with a similar task in an office building. Can the office property manager match the performance of the hotel industry?

The distance between current performance and the world's best defines the long-term improvement potential; the larger the difference the greater the management challenge. This distance is sometimes known as the 'stretch'. The test of a good business is when it takes on a stretching target and succeeds. On a benchmarking visit to the USA, BAA discovered that managers of particular high-rise office buildings were resolving the majority of property faults within 15 minutes. This compared with the BAA portfolio target of 80% within 48 hours. The stretch between these two targets was significant and prompted BAA to carry out a complete review of its processes and approach to service delivery in this area.

The company set itself, and subsequently achieved, the target of improving performance to a level where 95% of property faults anywhere on the airport estates are now resolved within 4 hours. The drive is now on to improve performance further.

The benchmarking of customer service performance is still a relatively undeveloped area both in the USA and the UK, but for those companies that aspire to be the best it is an essential ingredient for success.

SUMMARY

Turning a company into a business that has the customer as the focus of all its activities is nothing new, but the challenges within an industry as traditional as property should not be underestimated. Many companies have built up highly successful businesses through just such a philosophy but many others, such as Virgin, have started with a clean sheet of paper. Past baggage makes the task more difficult.

In the modern world a property company cannot rely on just a few top people to keep it healthy and growing. The complex nature of property management, and the threat of strong competition, means that there must be a systematic and rigorous approach to providing customers with what they want. For long-term success this must become a natural everyday part of the way an organization is managed. In this way, excellence can be maintained and is not reliant on one or two people at the top.

The BAA Property Challenge is a proven model for a customer focused property business, and the six Building Blocks offer companies a logical path to establishing such an organization.

Notes

1.   Sir John Egan, Chief Executive, BAA plc.
2.   Professor Ranko Bon, Head of Department of Construction Management and Engineering, The University of Reading (British Council for Offices Conference 1996).
3.   LaSalle Partners Management Limited, Mission Statement 1992.
4.   Pritchett, P. Ph.D (Dallas, Texas) (1996) 'Culture Shift: The Employee Handbook for Changing Corporate Culture' used with full permission of Pritchett & Associates, Inc.
5.   Hammer, M. and J. Champy (1993) *Re-engineering the Corporation: A Manifesto for Business Revolution* (London: Nicholas Brealey Publications).

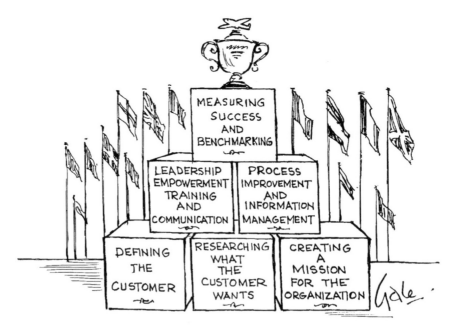

"BUILDING SUCCESS"

4 The Property Challenge Model

This chapter describes in more detail the first three of the Property Challenge Building Blocks:

- Defining the customer
- Researching what the customer wants
- Creating a mission for the organization

When considering each of them it is helpful to understand and remember the needs of the different stakeholder groups that must all be satisfied if a company is to maintain long-term success.

STAKEHOLDER GROUPS

The following are the five key stakeholders for a property owner:

Customers

Meeting the needs of tenants is central to establishing and maintaining a successful property-owning business.

Employees

If a company is adopting a new approach to the way tenants are viewed, its employees may be understandably sceptical about the change of style. They need to be convinced that this new way is for real and not just another management initiative that will flounder when the next one comes along. This needs to be done by involving staff in the shape and content of the mission statement and by helping them understand the good sense behind its objectives. The staff are also crucial in assisting a company understand the views of customers. Colleagues who may be indirectly involved in delivering service to customers must also be involved in the process of change. In this way they can understand the new business approach and will be prepared to support the efforts to improve service delivery.

Suppliers

If a company relies on suppliers to provide products and services to its customers, it is clearly essential that they too should understand any change in approach so that they can deliver the service standards the customers expect. Suppliers should have access to customer service feedback and be encouraged to learn from it and thereby improve performance.

Investors

The *raison d'être* for most commercial organizations is to increase share-holder value through revenue and capital growth, and a customer focused approach is the means to this end. As Will Carling noted:

> It is dangerous for members of a rugby team to look up at the scoreboard mid-way through a match. The reason I say this is that recognizing the score can make a player respond in a way that breaks away from a well-considered plan. The effect of thinking about the score, not about the processes of winning, is that the processes can be forgotten, to the ultimate detriment of the score.[1]
>
> (BAA plc, Property Staff Conference, 1996)

This is an interesting analogy for business; maintain the strategic focus and values of an organization and the result should be a successful financial scoreboard for the investors.

Community

Most buildings make a strong impact in their locality, through their architectural quality, the employment they provide and possibly the pollutants they emit. Property owners that choose to ignore their wider community responsibility will inevitably find the world moving against them as more-enlightened organizations take up the challenge to satisfy this important stakeholder group.

To summarize, seamless delivery of excellent service and value to customers is a prerequisite for financial success, but it is also necessary to satisfy the requirements of other stakeholder groups. Achieving this will be facilitated by establishing good two-way channels of communication to ensure continuous learning about the aspirations of all stakeholder groups.

BLOCK 1   DEFINING THE CUSTOMER

In a business such as property which has little track record of customer service, defining the customer is not as straightforward as it may seem. A property development and trading company might consider the funding institution or investment purchaser as its customer. Although these institutions are important stakeholders they are not customers, who are instead the end-users.

A customer could be defined as any organization that buys a product from a supplier but in the case of property management it is also helpful and relevant to consider each member of the tenant's staff as a customer. In a shopping centre the definition must extend beyond retail companies to individual shoppers. In this way, the landlord not only takes rightful responsibility for corporate occupiers but also for satisfying the needs of a wider group of people who are also vital to the landlord's prosperity.

Customer representatives also need to be well understood; these can range from the chief executive to the office manager, and the professional adviser to a tenant also has some of the characteristics of a customer. The definition of a customer is further complicated by the different perspectives from which customers view products; they will have very different needs in terms of cost, quality, facilities and location. The hotel sector provides a good example. The hotel business is highly competitive, especially during periods of slack demand, and, like in other property sectors, location is a factor although there are others.

Certainly, location is important to all the principal hotel market segments; business travellers, holiday-makers and leisure travellers, and conference delegates. The preferred location will, of course, be influenced by the purpose of the guest's visit. Some guests may be visiting clients in the financial district, others attending a conference at a convention centre, and holiday-makers intent on sightseeing, shopping and museum visits will wish to be near those places of interest.

But location is not the only factor that customers consider when selecting an hotel. Business travellers, for example, are probably travelling on expense accounts that allow a company president to stay in five-star hotels, senior managers in four-star hotels, and junior sales representatives in budget accommodation. In short, there are different classes of hotel based on customers' ability and willingness to pay for increasing levels of service, facilities and quality, as well as for a more desirable location.

This translates in the property sector into prospective tenants falling into different customer groups all looking for different types of service from a landlord's marketing team. The different groups with varying needs can only be understood by a landlord that regularly undertakes the necessary research. A landlord with a clear understanding of a customer group and its requirements will be better able to deliver the right quality at the right cost and thereby remain profitable.

BLOCK 2   RESEARCHING WHAT THE CUSTOMER WANTS

The property industry and particularly the sector responsible for managing property investments does not have a customer research-based culture. The research that is undertaken is often restricted to forecasting demand trends and the movement in capital values. Tenants are usually forgotten, and yet researching their needs and then delivering what they want will, in the long run, be central to the financial performance of a property investment.

Since the property recession of the late 1980s, the voice of the tenant has been heard more loudly. This has largely occurred because the tenant has been in a strong position during negotiations, with the landlord obliged to accede to the tenant's requirements in order to let property that would otherwise remain empty.

As night follows day, when the pendulum swings back in favour of the landlord many tenants will find that their landlords have lost their responsiveness. Such inconsistencies towards customers are not shown by a company that wishes to build a profitable long-term business. Companies that wish to remain constant in delivering good service and value to their customers will continue to research and continue to deliver what the customers are asking for in both good times and bad times.

"LISTENING TO THE CUSTOMER"

Customer surveys

The landlord must take the initiative to find out the level of customer satis-faction among a representative sample of customers. There are various ways of setting about this, such as:

- Face-to-face surveys
- Telephone surveys
- Postal questionnaires
- Focus groups
- Customer meetings/surgeries
- Informal out-of-office communication

Research is about obtaining accurate management information on issues that are important to customers in a way that can be relied upon to track performance over time. As long as these aims are achieved the landlord can choose any of the survey methods, depending on the circumstances.

Surveys are either quantitative or qualitative, but in order to first es-tablish and then regularly monitor the level of customer satisfaction quantitative surveys are necessary. At BAA plc, the main quantitative measurement tool is the annual tenant survey. This has been carried out by independent researchers since 1993 across a representative sample of tenants, weighted towards the decision-makers of BAA plc's more important customers.

Figure 4.1 shows some of the questions, which range from the detailed such as 'How do you rate the speed of response to account queries?' to the more general such as 'How do you rate the overall performance of BAA plc as a landlord?'.The tenants are asked to score the landlord's perfor-mance on a scale of 1 to 5, with 1 being very poor and 5 excellent.

Q7. Regarding personal contacts with BAA plc, how would you rate their dealings with account queries in terms of the ...

	Not applicable	Not yet encountered	Excellent	Good	Average	Poor	Very poor	Reason for Rating:
Speed of response	n/a	0	5	4	3	2	1	
Clarity of response	n/a	0	5	4	3	2	1	

Q23. How would you rate...

	No opinion	Excellent	Good	Average	Poor	Very poor	Reason for Rating:
Overall performance of BAA plc as Landlord	0	5	4	3	2	1	

Q24. How does this compare with the performance of other landlords with whom you have tenancies? (This would include other airports where you have accommodation as well as off airport locations).

	Not applicable	No opinion	Much Better	Better	Same	Worse	Much Worse	Why do you say that?
Other Landlords	n/a	0	5	4	3	2	1	

Q25. How would you rate the .....

	No opinion	Excellent	Good	Average	Poor	Very poor	Reason for Rating:
Overall value for money of the accom- modation?	0	5	4	3	2	1	

Q26. How does this compare with the value for money of accommodation at ...

	Not applicable	No opinion	Much Better	Better	Same	Worse	Much Worse	Reason for Rating:
Other airport locations (not operated by BAA plc)	n/a	0	5	4	3	2	1	
Off airport locations	n/a	0	5	4	3	2	1	

Q29. How has performance in the following areas changed over the last 12 months?

	Not applicable	No opinion	Much Better	Better	Same	Worse	Much Worse	Why do you say that?
Quality of accom- modation	n/a	0	5	4	3	2	1	
Communi- cations between BAA plc and your company	n/a	0	5	4	3	2	1	
Value for money	n/a	0	5	4	3	2	1	

Figure 4.1   Examples of tenant survey questions

This survey has enabled BAA plc to focus management action on areas which command low scores, and to put renewed efforts into areas where scores are not improving or may have slipped back. Without the survey it would not be possible to measure performance in the eyes of customers, and if a company cannot measure performance it cannot improve it.

The tenant survey is directed at decision-makers who may be based in a head office, but it is equally important to obtain survey information from the occupiers of buildings. They may not make lease renewal decisions but they will certainly influence those decisions. The BAA plc occupier survey asks a more detailed set of questions about a particular building, such as those listed in Figure 4.2.

Q4. How would you rate the ... (circle the appropriate rating)

	Not Applicable	Excellent	Good	Average	Poor	Very poor	Reasons for Rating:
Quality of fixtures/ decor in common areas	n/a	5	4	3	2	1	
Cleanliness of common areas	n/a	5	4	3	2	1	
Flexibility of space	n/a	5	4	3	2	1	
Heating	n/a	5	4	3	2	1	

Q8. In their initial response to faults and repairs, how would you rate BAA plc staff's ...

	Not yet Encountered	Excellent	Good	Average	Poor	Very poor	Reasons for Rating:
Speed of Response	0	5	4	3	2	1	
Style of Response	0	5	4	3	2	1	

Q13. How have the following areas changed over the last 12 months?

	Don't know	Much Improved	Improved	Same	Worse	Much worse	Reasons for Rating
Quality of Accommodation	0	5	4	3	2	1	
Quality of service	0	5	4	3	2	1	
Quality of maintenance services	0	5	4	3	2	1	

Q19. In your day-to-day dealings with your property contacts within BAA plc, how would you rate...

	Don't know	Excellent	Good	Average	Poor	Very poor	Reasons for Rating
The ease of contacting the 'right' person	0	5	4	3	2	1	
Their speed of response	0	5	4	3	2	1	
Their style of response	0	5	4	3	2	1	

Figure 4.2   Examples of occupier survey questions

The occupier survey is carried out by BAA plc staff and, because the interviews are informal, there is an opportunity for the property manager to understand the reasons behind the customers' responses – all good qualitative information. This is also an ideal opportunity for the occupiers to talk about the things that are important to them; the new services they might require, the value of shared facilities or the need for new space. The formality of a survey gives hard quantitative information and the informality gives vital qualitative information and new ideas that can be used to improve customer service and secure tenant loyalty.

The occupier survey also played an important part in helping to change the culture of BAA plc's property managers, who previously had never thought to ask customers if they were satisfied with the service provided. The occupier survey provided the means for property managers to break the ice with their customers, to start talking about things that were important to them and to face up to the fact that improvements were needed.

Improved performance through measurement

If a management team has been acting in the same way for many years, it is unrealistic to expect wholesale change at the flick of a switch. Nevertheless, the provision of measurable customer feedback can have an energizing effect on such management. Few people go to work to do a bad job; customer information shows what action they can take to do a good job.

Measuring standards also enables management targets to be set, and achieving these goals is motivating. A well-motivated management team is more likely to be proactive and creative in finding ways not only to satisfy customers but also to grow the business on the back of this customer focused success.

Sometimes there is a need for more in-depth qualitative information, focused on a particular subject. If it is a difficult or sensitive issue, it is often best to bring in an independent facilitator to run a focus group so that no stone is left unturned in seeking out the real issues. For best results a focus group should be limited to 10 customer representatives, but if a broader sample is needed then additional focus groups can be organized. With the consent of the members of a focus group comments can be recorded on video. The tape can then be played back to the manager responsible for a process who may have had no idea that a customer felt so strongly about a particular issue.

Perhaps the best way to research customers is through everyday communication. At every level throughout an organization, staff should be encouraged to talk to their customers about their businesses, and to find out if the landlord's service delivery can be improved or if there are other services that the customer needs. If this can be done in an informal atmosphere over a cup of coffee then so much the better. These efforts at seeking feedback have a double benefit – they show that a company cares about its customer, but they also build relationships which help to ensure that issues are resolved before they become conflicts.

In a different business sector, Texaco relies heavily on customer feedback to discover what its customers want:

> Through surveys, regular customer panel meetings, and the Mystery Motorist campaign we are able to obtain regular feedback on areas where we are doing well with our service stations and where improvements are necessary. There is also the national freephone customer service line which enables any customer, at any Texaco service station anywhere in the UK, to speak to our customer services team for free.
>
> It is estimated that over 2000 customers call every month. All calls are monitored to provide Texaco with accurate information as to what the customer wants. Extensive qualitative and quantitative analysis is required on a perpetual basis if you wish to make a real contribution to improving relations with your customers. You can then take this information to the point of sale, which may be at the service station itself, or to the appropriate department within Texaco, in order that changes can be made.
>
> The Mystery Motorist campaign is a case in point. Every year a mystery motorist visits every Texaco service station in the UK, to measure how successful Texaco has been in meeting motorists' requirements.[2]
>
> (Taylor, *Quality: Total Customer Service*, 1992)

Customers are becoming more demanding, organizations more diverse and issues more complex. Although seeking accurate management information from customers is somewhat alien to the property industry, it is as relevant there as it is to a company like Texaco.

Communication

It is sometimes easy to fall into the trap of surveys becoming a one-way road with no feedback to the customer. A customer survey, with a supplier carefully listening to concerns, can raise expectations of improved service and value which in reality may take time to deliver; the issues may involve complex processes that cannot be improved overnight. It is therefore important to establish good two-way communication so that the tenant knows that their views are being acted upon, as well as the likely pace and scale of change.

Particularly where a group of customers is relatively small, even annual surveys can cause 'survey fatigue', especially if improvements are slow to come. Fresh ways of collecting information need to be found so that the research is still statistically valid but collected in a way that is a pleasure to the customer rather than a mundane, almost mechanical process. The greatest danger of all is the disenchantment that will result if a landlord takes up a tenant's time for research and then is unwilling to address the points raised.

BLOCK 3   CREATING A MISSION FOR THE ORGANIZATION

An organization is made up of many people with individual characteristics and views about how the business should be run. These people may have different perspectives about the objectives and values of the company unless clarity of purpose is given to each and every one of them. If the whole team pulls in the same direction, the energy created will drive the company forward to achieve its objectives. The reverse is the case if the mission of the company is unclear.

In a business with many sites, such as a property investment portfolio, the importance of giving managers clarity of purpose cannot be overestimated. In considering further how this can be done the following questions arise:

- What is a mission?
- Why develop a mission?
- When to develop a mission?
- How to develop a mission?

What is a mission?

A mission statement sets out the core objective of an organization, the values that will be maintained and the methods by which the objective will be achieved.

For a mission to be successful, there are three requisites:

- it must support the business needs;
- it must be logical and easy to understand; and
- staff must be involved in its development.

A mission statement should make reference to the key drivers for success and these would certainly include quality, service, cost, people and ethics. If a mission statement is applicable to an airport-owning company, a retailer, a car service centre, a power generator and distributor, and an express delivery service, then why not to a property owner?

The central theme of a mission should be simple, as in the case of BAA plc:

> Our mission is to make BAA plc the most successful airport company in the world through:
> Always focusing on our customers' needs and safety
> Achieving continuous improvements in the costs and quality of all our processes and services
> Enabling our employees to give of their best.

The full BAA plc mission statement is shown in the Appendix.

The retailer Bhs has also decided to keep it simple:

> Bhs will be the first choice store for today's woman and family. We are committed to service, quality, harmony, innovation and excitement to deliver value in all that we do. We will succeed by being a focused organisation in dynamic partnership with our customers, suppliers and each one of us.[3]
> (Bhs plc Mission Statement)

If the words 'store for dressing the modern woman and family' were replaced by 'supplier of buildings for industry', then the mission could be owned with pride by a property owner.

The mission statement of Kwik-Fit (GB) could apply equally to a property owner:

> At Kwik-fit the most important person is the customer and it must be the aim of us all to give 100% customer satisfaction 100% of the time. Our continued success depends on the loyalty of our customers. We are commited to a policy of offering them the best value for money with a fast and courteous and professional service. We offer the highest-quality products and guarantees. We at Kwik-Fit recognize that our people are our most valuable asset. The Kwik-Fit people at our centres are the all-important contact with the customers and they are the key to the success of the Kwik-Fit group.[4]   (Kwik-Fit (GB) Ltd, Mission Statement)

Scottish Hydro-Electric places maximum emphasis on customers but includes all stakeholder groups in its mission:

> Hydro-Electric's highest priority is delivering exceptional customer satisfaction. It also aims to be recognized as an outstanding Company by its customers, staff, shareholders, community and suppliers.[5]
>
> (Scottish Hydro-Electric plc, Misson Statement, 1992)

Again, this is a mission which could be applicable equally to a property owner.

A landlord genuinely wishing to work in partnership with a tenant must understand the objectives, values and culture of the tenant company. A good way of starting this process is to read the company's mission which in some cases, such as DHL Worldwide, will be very detailed:

> DHL will become the acknowledged global leader in the express delivery of documents and packages. Leadership will be achieved by establishing the industry standards of excellence for quality and service and by maintaining the lowest cost position relative to our service commitment in all markets of the world. Achievement of the mission requires:
>
> > absolute dedication to understanding and fulfilling our customers' needs with the appropriate mix of service, reliability, products and price for each customer; ensuring the long-term success of the business through profitable growth and reinvestment of earnings; an environment that rewards achievement, enthusiasm and team spirit and which offers each person in DHL superior opportunities for personal development and growth; a state of the art worldwide information network for customer billing, tracking, tracing and management information/communications; allocation of resources consistent with the recognition that we are one worldwide business; and a professional organization able to maintain local initiative and local decision making while working together within a centrally managed network.
>
> The evolution of our business into new services, markets or products will be completely driven by our single-minded commitment to anticipating and meeting the changing needs of our customers.[6]
>
> (DHL Worldwide, Mission Statement, 1997)

A property manager who can 'get inside the head' of a tenant organization such as DHL Worldwide, is well placed to be responsive to the occupier in a relevant and value-adding way.

Mission statements are often directed towards satisfying customers, but the unwritten objective is to direct the skills of a management team in a way that adds to shareholder value. Satisfied customers are essential, but this must be achieved in a way and at a cost that also provides acceptable shareholder returns. The mission statement can provide the focus to ensure that this challenging task is accomplished.

Why develop a mission?

Almost every company facing major changes in its business will find a mission a key instrument in achieving those changes. It is a description of what the company is seeking to do and how the aims will be achieved. It provides an invaluable rallying point for staff in developing their understanding of the issues which are fundamental to the future success of their company. As a result, it provides a unity of purpose for the staff at all levels in the organization, as well as for external suppliers.

It gives everyone within a company direction and guidance about how to act in any particular circumstance and provides senior management and staff with the confidence that the organization's philosophy will be consistent throughout the company and over time.

When to develop a mission?

A mission is developed as a result of business needs, and can have the greatest impact and benefit when a company is going through radical change, either in its products or its culture. Once a change is understood to be necessary and the company devises a strategy for the business then the mission is helpful in articulating the strategy to all staff, suppliers and, sometimes, customers.

Although the objectives and values of a company are unlikely to change, the emphasis and method of delivery can and should evolve over time to meet changing customer requirements and business practices. Any changes should only be made with the close involvement of staff and these occasions also provide the opportunity to underscore the main thrust of the company as outlined in the mission statement.

How to develop a mission?

The leader of an organization is usually the catalyst for developing a mission. However, the most successful missions will not be those which are handed down from on high, but ones which are developed through two-way communication with staff. Suppliers and customers should also play their part.

Reaching a point where all influential stakeholders help to develop a mission can be a lengthy process, but it will be worth it. Just as in the construction of a building, it is sensible to spend sufficient time on the design and planning stages to ensure that all those involved are satisfied that the best design has been arrived at. Changes of mind are expensive on a construction project but even more so for a company whose mission turns out to have flaws.

The development of the mission is an important process in itself because it can help release energy, create ideas and enable people to understand the need for change. This can be done through presentations, seminars, focus groups, and any other means of communication which suits the company. Through this process, staff can be given the chance to understand the opportunities that will be opened up by doing things in a new way and the threats to the business if the traditions of the past become further entrenched. Staff then have the information from which they can make a choice; either to keep things as they are or to join their colleagues in an invigorated and sustainable enterprise.

Before the final version of a mission statement is signed off it is good practice to run with a draft for 6 to 12 months so that any minor adjustments can be made. The final version should then be agreed and communicated as widely as possible.

In the case of BAA plc property, the driving force for change was an understanding that the property business had not sufficiently met the needs of customers, was losing market share, and consequently ran the risk of under-performing unless action was taken. So the principal statement of the BAA plc Property Challenge is 'to develop fully our property potential, and build a world-class property business'. BAA plc's first intention was to run the best-managed airport estate in the world, but the longer-term aim was this higher and wider aspiration.

The strategy adopted to deliver the Property Challenge was driven entirely by the voice of the customer. Having learnt what the customers wanted, BAA plc identified three action areas. The Property Challenge set out to offer customers: hospitality and quality, value for money and choice.

BAA plc linked the principal statement and the three action areas with four further points which indicate to all staff and suppliers what is expected of them to help deliver the Property Challenge. These following points focused on the most important issues which were identified and agreed through the two-way communication process with staff:

- Treating tenants as valued customers and always focusing on their needs and safety.
- Continuously improving the value for money enjoyed by customers.

- Using information technology to help deliver improved customer service.
- Enabling employees to give of their best and involving them in shaping how BAA plc changes.

As in the case of BAA plc, there is no reason why there should not be a company-wide mission and also one for a business unit, indeed this can add focus and relevance, but it is equally important that the missions are dovetailed together in a way that is complementary and adds strength to both.

Three of the six Property Challenge Building Blocks have so far been described and at this point the customer has been defined, customer needs identified and objectives and values agreed. The next Building Block, leadership, empowerment, training and communication, is dealt with in Chapter 5. Chapter 6 covers process improvement and Chapter 7 deals with information management and benchmarking.

Notes

1. Will Carling, former England rugby union captain, at the BAA plc Property Staff Conference 1996.
2. Taylor, L.K. (1992) *Quality: Total Customer Service* (London: Century Business).
3. Bhs plc, Mission Statement.
4. Kwik-Fit (GB) Ltd, Mission Statement.
5. Scottish Hydro-Electric plc, Mission Statement 1992.
6. DHL Worldwide, Mission Statement 1997.

5 Leadership, Empowerment, Training and Communication

MOBILISING PEOPLE FOR CHANGE

Achieving a truly customer focused organization means mobilising everyone in the organization to achieve a common goal. In many cases this will mean a real shift in culture or 'the way we do things round here'. It involves effective leadership of a team that is well-directed, motivated and trained. This is the fourth Building Block. Senior managers can play a leading role, but the philosophy will only be convincing if it is understood and practised right through the organization, from the operational property manager to the chief executive.

This chapter considers the importance of effective leadership and looks at how peoples' motivation to give of their best can be released and harnessed. Training is also covered in some depth because it is an area where the property industry has under invested. The training available to most practising property managers has been broadly restricted to technical issues, many to do with securing maximum gain from the tenant. Training is often central to the formula for success in profitable international companies and yet in the property industry training has a low priority, and training in the softer skills of customer service is almost non-existent.

LEADERSHIP

In property a customer is buying both a product and a service, and there are numerous interfaces between the supplier and customer, spread over a long period. These cover a range of different issues and will probably involve people from different departments, dealing with diverse issues from account queries to lift breakdowns, and from legal interpretation to window cleaning.

These interfaces or 'moments of truth' create good, bad or indifferent experiences for the customer and lead the way to the customer's overall

THE PROPERTY MANAGER WHO FORGOT TO MENTION LEADERSHIP,
EMPOWERMENT, TRAINING AND COMMUNICATION. "

opinion of the supplier. This opinion will normally influence the future decision on whether to repurchase.

The key to good customer service is the attitude and competence of the front-line staff, but it does not stop there. Who influences them? Who influences what they can and cannot do? Who establishes and perpetuates the processes by which they are required to work? And who rewards them? The answer in all cases is the management. The commitment to the delivery of customer service must start from the very top, and for this reason the leadership of any organization plays a vital role in the implementation of change.

The leader's role is to ensure that the business objectives and priorities are clearly identified and expressed in terms that are understood by all those who are important to the organization's success. A chief executive is, in a sense, the guardian of a company's mission and must believe that the objectives, values and methods of the company are ones that can be promoted and defended with enthusiasm and even passion. Any less commitment will soon become a message that the boss is not keen to change, so why should anyone else be?

Leadership must be consistent and by example (Binney and Williams, *Leaning into the Future*, 1995). The greatest single influence in any change process is the example set by people who command respect and have influence. Employees judge a manager's commitment to any changes 10% on what they say and 90% on what they do.[1]

Binney and Williams describe a model in their book in which successful leaders of change have combined contradictory abilities:

> to lead and learn, to provide direction whilst allowing autonomy, and to be forthright yet prepared to listen[2]
>
> (Binney and Williams, *Leaning into the Future*, 1995)

The three elements of leading, empowering and training are all there.

EMPOWERING THE TEAM TO DELIVER

It is clear from the Binney–Williams model that leadership, whilst vital, is not enough. Leaders cannot do everything; they are reliant on their colleagues who must be empowered to enable them to lead by example and, in turn, to empower their staff to do likewise. Only if everyone is pulling in the same direction can change be implemented efficiently.

People's characters are naturally dependent on their culture, education, influences and experience. These factors, or the lack of them, for better or worse, will have made them how they are and may well result in their having unrealized potential. A good leader who enjoys people and has a sensitivity towards them will allow each and every person to unlock their talents and reach their full potential. As well as being more rewarding for both manager and managed, the energy that is released can then be directed towards achieving the goals of the company.

A well-trained and motivated manager can take on greater responsibility, make larger financial decisions and react with speed and confidence to customer requests. This improves service levels and reduces costs by cutting out unnecessary approvals. These two things are central to achieving profitability.

The question to ask is 'How can well-skilled and motivated managers be enabled to reach their full potential and thereby add most value to the company?' There are a number of ways of answering the question but the central tenet is about empowering people to do well.

> Empowerment is what happens when managers give up being 'in control' and give power to people, treating them as individuals and enabling them to put in their best effort. Empowerment results in people going beyond both what is expected of them and what they believe themselves.[3]
>
> (TQM International Ltd, *Motivation and Empowerment*, 1996)

Empowerment is a mental attitude that cannot be gifted to someone; it is a sense of freedom, born of knowledge and confidence, which can be encouraged within the individual but most significantly can only be achieved at the wish of the individual.

Empowerment is a philosophy that demands:

that employees, the life-blood of the business, take a more dynamic role in the day-to-day performance of their duties. This may mean finding new improved ways of working, taking more job responsibility, using initiative or making balanced decisions.

Whatever form this involvement takes, it provides the vitality essential in a growing organization and it is everyone's responsibility to harness this potential. After all, who has greater insight into a system than the people who are involved in running it?[4]   (Sir John Egan, 'Empowerment', 1996)

In essence, companies must move from a traditional approach to an empowered one (TQM International Ltd, *Motivation and Empowerment*, 1996), and Figure 5.1[5] provides some of the pointers to these two ways of doing things. An employee with an empowered state of mind experiences feelings of:

- control over how the job will be performed;
- awareness of the context in which the work is performed and how it fits the big picture;
- accountability for personal work output;
- shared responsibility for the unit and organizational performance; and
- sharing in the distribution of rewards based on individual and collective performance.

Empowerment cannot be bought, nor does it happen overnight, but has to be created and developed to meet the needs of the business. The single biggest requirement is mutual trust between managers and their direct staff, combined with a change in the working relationship. Managers will not enable empowerment by remaining traditional bosses with a strong technical skills base; they must instead develop other, softer skills that help their people reach their full potential.

The manager must become a skilled coach, using experience to assist others in the development of their own talents. The role of the coach requires managers to disperse decision-making and to loosen reins, to be open, and prepared to listen and learn and to promote two-way feedback. For many managers this can be a difficult and threatening change, yet giving away power changes the nature of leadership; it becomes more subtle and certainly more enjoyable.

Conversely, it is also difficult for the staff who receive greater authority. For them the change increases the risk of making mistakes, it places an obligation on them to acquire knowledge, and it puts pressure on them to use their judgement and to come up with creative solutions to problems.

These issues can, at least in part, be overcome if a clear framework is created which both managers and staff understand and work within. In enabling all employees to take an active decision-making role, it is important that there are recognizable boundaries. To achieve this BAA plc uses a traffic-light analogy, with red, amber and green zones:

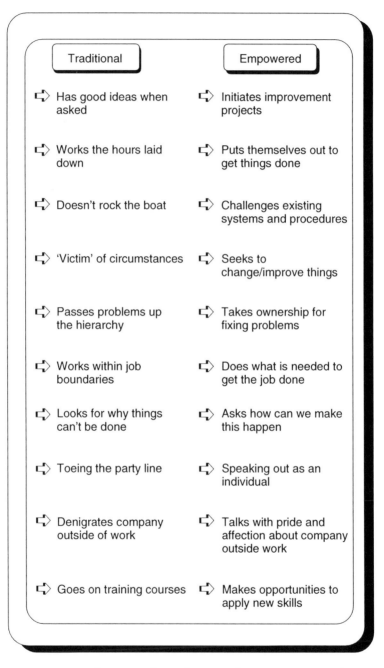

Figure 5.1   Moving from a traditional approach to an empowered approach (Source: TQM International Ltd, Motivation and Empowerment, 1996)

- *Green zone* Each member of the team knows the areas where they are expected to be responsible for making decisions and where there is freedom to act without approval.
- *Amber zone* Employees require some consultation with management either before or after taking action. The action could have taken place to provide a fast customer response but another department might be affected.
- *Red zone* Staff should only make decisions after consulting their managers, for instance on potential infringements of health and safety requirements.

One way of assessing the extent to which an organization is empowered is to watch how front-line staff respond to problems they encounter. An owner-type response indicates a real feeling of empowerment.

In his book *On Great Service – A Framework for Action*, Leonard L. Berry describes an empowerment model which divides the organization into three layers, each of which is required to 'think' and to operate as a team. The model identifies the different roles of the groups:

- Top management – sets direction and establishes a culture of achievement
- Middle management – coaches achievement and removes obstacles
- Front-line servers – manage themselves in creating value for their customers

Empowerment enables a company to tap into the creativity, intellect and emotional energy of nearly everyone in the organization, not just those in the executive suite.[6]   (Berry, *On Great Service*, 1995)

But empowerment cannot be created in a vacuum, it requires first and foremost that the objectives, values and methods of the organization are understood and communicated to the staff in terms that they can all understand and associate with. How else can they be expected to make appropriate decisions? As Sir John Egan commented:

We have actively encouraged positive employee involvement and decision making within acceptable risk levels, and this has dramatically improved both customer service and employee satisfaction.[7]

(Sir John Egan, 'Empowerment', 1996)

The benefits of faster customer response times and reduced internal costs can be considerable but there are risks. First, that employees will make poor decisions or, worse, fail to make any decisions. Second, there is potential for organizational change and staff turnover because not everyone will be comfortable when encouraged to take on greater responsibility. Third, there is generally a need for increased investment in training and education.

It is the third point which cannot be avoided, partly because training and education are the means to overcome the first two risks.

TRAINING

Training for sport, contest or occupation is normally intended to meet a specific and current need; in other words, what the individual needs to know or be able to do to complete a task or to do a particular job. The belief that training is only something you need to undertake before you start a new job, or before you can qualify as a professional, has pervaded the property business for far too long. Training is an ongoing process and not just a series of courses.

Training is only part of the learning equation; the other part is development. If training is about the here and now, development, which can be defined as a stage of growth or advancement, is about enabling individuals to cope with the future, to enable them to develop their careers and to handle organizational change. Any organization that strives to achieve sustainable success must have a strategy which provides both training and development opportunities, an approach now commonly referred to as continuous learning.

Well-trained and adaptable people are the key to sustainable success in the fast-moving and increasingly-competitive global market in which organizations must change to meet new challenges. Although most professions do now acknowledge the need for continuing training, the traditional focus is on technical training and stops short of embracing the concept of lifelong learning, and the need for companies to become learning organizations.

Education and training can therefore no longer be regarded as issues of cost, but as preconditions for competitive success. This applies to the property industry as it does to any other. The average property owner or manager has put too little resource into training people in the wider management skills that would be of value in another industry. Yet the job-for-life culture is fast disappearing, so how will companies be able to secure the right people if they are not able to provide them with job-for-life security? The solution for both parties is a new understanding of work, one where the employer supports and promotes a learning culture and the employees accept and adopt a learning habit. This introduces a new concept – careers for life – that satisfies both the employee's requirement for security and the employer's requirement for an efficient, flexible and appropriately-skilled workforce.

The Royal Society of Arts in its recent *Tomorrow's Company* inquiry (1995)[8] suggested that organizations should have:

- a disciplined framework for personal learning plans, including learning targets and a mentoring system;
- a board-level focus on learning;

- a reward system linked to learning achievement; and
- a systematic approach to becoming a learning organization.

For organizations the key benefits of learning are that it enables the organization to prepare for the future, and it maximizes the potential of its people. For employees, the key benefits are that it maintains their employability, and it enables them to maximize their potential.

The first step to becoming a learning organization is obtaining genuine commitment at the top. Leaders must take ownership of the approach and ensure that there is no gap between the rhetoric and practice. Any gap will encourage scepticism and undermine morale.

In a fast-changing world, companies need to be able to respond quickly to new competitive pressures. It is the people in the organization who, if trained to do so, can respond successfully in a positive and innovative way. The ability to do this is a vital and fundamental output of the learning process. Looked at another way, people must be trained and involved in helping to shape the way their organizations change.

TRAINING TO ACHIEVE THE BUSINESS STRATEGY

The strategic goals of an organization are the objectives which are set out to meet the requirements of stakeholder groups such as shareholders, customers, employees, the community and business partners. If all the stakeholders are contented then there is a good chance that the business will be financially successful and sustainable. To facilitate the achievement of the strategic goals there needs to be a good understanding of the skills required. This could be called the 'business competency' framework and will be specific to the organization.

As an example, within BAA plc this framework consists of four competencies generic to all parts of the business, including operations, property, retail and construction. The competencies are:

- Meeting customer needs profitably
- Managing the business process
- Leading people
- Self-management

BAA plc's property training strategy is built within this business competency framework but has also been designed to address its property mission statement priorities:

- Hospitality and quality
- Choice
- Value for money

The development of a training strategy needs to be carefully considered and structured so that it helps define the company's strategic goals. Set out below is an outline of the six-stage process that BAA plc went through to produce its property training strategy.

Stage 1   setting the standards

A series of indicators, or standards, were established for each of the four competencies. For example, the standards for 'meeting customer needs profitably' are:

- Dealing with customers with integrity
- Knowing the product, the market and the facilities on offer
- Taking an active interest in customers' businesses in order to understand and satisfy their needs
- Selling the benefits of the value for money package
- Taking ownership of customers' problems
- Responding speedily and effectively to customers
- Understanding customers' priorities

Stage 2   initial analysis of learning priorities

Having established a mission and understood the business competencies, Stage 2 was to determine the generic learning priorities to achieve business aims and meet individual needs. The analysis identified four learning priority areas:

Leadership

BAA plc recognized that to achieve excellence in customer service, effective training in leadership was essential, and that the leadership style must reflect the following characteristics:

- Leaders must promote empowerment
- They should have a coaching rather than an instructional style of management
- Leaders need to actively seek and be receptive to feedback from their teams on their personal style
- They need to have the ability to translate business strategy into tactics and communicate the strategy to a variety of audiences, such as internal business partners and clients
- Leaders should act as role models and set the image of the strategy

Process

Moving from a traditional property management business to a customer focused one requires people to understand and re-engineer business processes to make them easy to operate and to ensure that they consistently meet customer expectations in a timely manner and at an appropriate cost. This required training to:

- Equip staff to participate or lead process reviews
- Ensure an understanding of the processes and how continuous review and improvement contribute to business success
- Explain the role and importance of teams in process reviews

Information technology (IT)

The analysis of processes confirmed that IT was vital to support the introduction of new or improved processes. This required all employees:

- To be competent in using software
- To be able to access data and translate it into useful information for the business
- To be able to identify and exploit opportunities for utilizing new technology to improve business efficiency

Service delivery

The analysis identified that to achieve excellent service delivery all staff need to have appropriate professional knowledge to enable them to make customer focused business decisions. The objective was to ensure staff understand the key elements of the BAA plc property business and the role of property within the overall airport business.

Stage 3   identifying the skills

Once the learning priorities had been identified and understood the next stage was to determine the skills that people need. The question asked was 'What would a perfect employee be like?' Skill requirements were broken down into three categories; core business skills, behavioural skills, and technical skills.

Core business skills

These are skills specific to individual organizations. They are the foundation skills that everyone needs in order to play a full part in the day-to-day running of a company. This knowledge need not be expert in all areas, but the person does need to have a good understanding of how different parts of the business operate so as to ensure well-founded decisions. Silos of knowledge lead to decisions being made on the basis of a narrow functional view and this can lead to expensive mistakes.

Behavioural skills

Good levels of knowledge are important but if the person facing a customer does not have matching interpersonal skills, customer relations can be damaged. For employees to operate most effectively, they need other abilities such as:

- Analytical skills including innovation, problem-solving and attention to detail
- Interpersonal skills such as leadership, interpersonal style, team-playing, empathy and persuasion
- Personal skills of vision, planning, drive with commitment, integrity, commercial insight and organizational awareness.

Technical skills

These are specific skills that staff need for their particular function to ensure that they are equipped to deliver the objectives of the company in a safe way. It is traditionally this third area that is the focus of training programmes within the property profession.

Stage 4   matching skill sets with priorities

Employees' skill sets then needed to be considered in relation to the business strategy priorities and competency standards identified earlier. A simple matrix can help summarize the requirements as shown in Table 5.1.

Stage 5   establishing the gap

By this stage, the following had been identified:

- The standards required
- The corporate learning priorities
- The skills needed
- The required match between skills and standards

The next stage was to compare what was required against the skills and abilities of the existing team. In other words, to assess the actual learning required to help people deliver the strategic goals of the company.

Table 5.1 A matrix for comparing business strategy priorities with competency standards

Business priority: hospitality and quality
Competency: meeting customer needs profitably

STANDARDS	COMPETENCIES				
	Core business	Analytical	Interpersonal	Personal	Technical
Dealing with integrity		X	X	X	
Knowing the product on offer	X				X
Taking active interest in customers' business	X		X	X	X
Selling the benefits of the value-for-money package	X	X	X	X	X
Taking ownership of customers' problems		X	X	X	
Responding speedily and efficiently		X	X	X	X
Understanding the customers' business priorities	X	X			

There are several ways of assessing this, including the use of performance management, development centres, workshops, individual self-assessment and observation. This is the ideal opportunity to help people understand both the personal and business imperatives for continuous learning.

Once the existing skill base has been established, it can be contrasted with the skills required and whatever is missing is the skills gap. The skills gap should determine the priorities for training.

Stage 6   filling the gap

At this stage it is worth remembering that different people will respond in different ways to learning, and what is right for one person may not be so for another. Few would disagree that the most effective means of learning is by experience but, as this is not always possible or practical, there are a range of other methods that can be used to suit the circumstances.

The methods include internal and external courses, seminars, secondments, shadowing, study tours, job swaps, distance learning, group workshops, mentoring and coaching, and work experience. The selection of the most appropriate method for the individual or group concerned is almost as important as the skills content. In each case careful thought needs to be given to why the individual needs training, how they learn best and what they will be expected to do once trained.

Delivering a property training strategy

It will be different for every company, depending on their size and resources, but BAA plc has a central team which provides training and development programmes in both core business skills and behavioural skills. The responsibility for the development and delivery of less-generic skills programmes rests with the individual BAA plc businesses.

Core business skills

This is an internal BAA plc course for senior managers, designed to develop all-round competence in core skills and to ensure an understanding of the business, its drivers, pressures and goals. The programme is modular; the core module is mandatory, other modules are optional and it is top managers who provide the training.

The core module focuses on business management and in particular on process improvement, managing change and empowerment. Support modules focus specifically on BAA plc business areas such as airport operations, property, retail, project process improvement, international, safety, corporate strategy, financial management and IT.

Behavioural skills

This is an internal five-day course focusing on the BAA plc mission statement, personal development and leadership. Subjects covered include the company culture and the implications for change, the changing role of the manager, continuous improvement, quality management, and constructive conflict.

Everyone who attends receives feedback on their performance as a manager, based on a questionnaire issued before the course where the views of their manager, peers and those who report to them are sought – 360 degree feedback. This is always enlightening, and sometimes painful. So as to be relevant to the objectives of the company, the questions in the questionnaire are grouped under the core competency headings of meeting customer needs profitably, managing the business process, leading people and self-management. Managers can then compare their results with the average results of all managers who have been through the process before them – including managers from other companies in other industries.

From the feedback and comparative information, managers are able to identify their behavioural skills development needs.

Property skills

To support the more general training and meet the particular needs of people responsible for property, BAA plc has developed an in-house training programme known as Property Prospects.

> The main objective is not just to provide people with technical skills and knowledge, but to demonstrate by means of practical exercises how they are expected to apply this back in the workplace. The courses are designed to help them learn and demonstrate their understanding of that learning.[9]
> (Paul Le Marquand, Assistant Group Property Director, BAA plc, 1996)

The programme consists of 15 modules, on subjects such as property management, service charges, development, health and safety, business planning and marketing. The idea is to ensure that everyone, from whatever department, has the opportunity to learn about the whole property business. This helps to ensure that customers are provided with a predictable, seamless service at all levels and across all functions.

The principles behind the programme are:

- All modules include case studies and project work based, where possible, on real examples
- All modules take the perspective of the customer
- Each module is aimed at the needs of the business
- The tutor for each module is a senior member of the property team and an acknowledged expert. This principle of using internal expertise is embodied within the tag-line for the programme – 'sharing our skills'

- Modules usually last no longer than a day
- Clear objectives are set for each module and criteria are established by the course tutor
- The experience is challenging and stretching but not overwhelming
- All modules are supported by written hand-outs for future reference
- All modules are attended by a range of people from different locations and the maximum number on any course is 20
- All modules include an assignment to be completed after the course
- The tutors assess the completed assignments and provide individual feedback

This approach is intended to unlock the potential of staff and improve the quality and range of their skills, whilst at the same time providing senior managers with an opportunity to develop their leadership skills by taking responsibility for particular modules.

Benefits to BAA plc of the training strategy

For every process there is at least one value-adding output and ultimately this must be the reason why the process exists. Training and development processes should not be any different. The overriding objective for BAA plc is that the training strategy should contribute towards the achievement of the group's mission statement, specifically 'enabling our employees to give of their best'.

There are a number of specific output benefits and these are summarized below:

Enhanced team working

Attendance by staff from different locations and functions allows cross-fertilization of ideas and fosters communication and team working.

Improved business success, increased efficiency, productivity and profit

A skilled workforce with shared objectives and an enhanced understanding of the business processes places less demand on management, reduces bureaucracy and is able to contribute considerably more to achieving the objectives of the organization.

Increased employee motivation

It would be rare indeed for someone to go to work in the morning with the intention of doing a bad job, but lack of skills obviously leads to poor performance. Just as bad is the frustration and demotivation that can result if people feel that they have not been given the opportunity to learn the skills to do the job.

People can also be protective towards their technical knowledge, feeling that sharing it somehow reduces their own importance to the company, thus making their position less secure. When the sharing of knowledge is reciprocal this threat is reduced or removed and the organization benefits from a team that has unlocked its full potential through the individual members sharing their skills and knowledge.

Innovation from within

It is a human characteristic when learning that we challenge the information we are receiving, even if it is done subconsciously. Often this elicits the question 'This may be a stupid question but why do we...?' This is the start of greater understanding which stimulates new thinking and innovation. After all, it is the person being trained who is the hands-on expert, but if learning can release creativity then financial benefits should follow.

Personal growth opportunities

Most employees know how fast the world is changing and understand how the nature of employment is developing rapidly. They understand, and are concerned about, the end of 'jobs for life', and may feel unqualified for the concept of 'careers for life' which may well involve moving to another industry. This, combined with individual ambition, places an obligation on any company that aspires to be a good employer to provide a framework for personal growth. A modular learning programme is part of this framework.

Qualifications

There is a view that if a company invests in a person's learning, for example by supporting an MBA programme, then that person becomes more mobile, to the potential disadvantage of the company. This upside-down thinking ignores the added value a person can give following such a learning programme. It also fails to see the very healthy longer-term challenge that a well-trained employee will make by saying 'Can you provide me with a fulfilling job that enables me to reach my full potential?' If the company is unable to answer 'yes', then the person would surely be best advised to look for fulfilment elsewhere.

At BAA plc, the completion of 15 Property Prospects modules earns an internal diploma, but to give this external recognition it is hoped, in the context of a wider programme, to secure university accreditation.

Succession planning

All organizations need to plan ahead to ensure that they are effectively resourced for the future. A well-managed training programme will facilitate succession planning by allowing people to enhance their knowledge and to demonstrate a desire and ability to progress. Senior managers running courses also have the opportunity to spot new and emerging talent.

INDIVIDUAL PERFORMANCE AND DEVELOPMENT

It can be said that each of us asks four basic questions of our manager and our company. The questions are:

- What is expected of me?
- What help do I need to succeed?
- Will I be rewarded fairly for my own contribution and the contribution I have made to the team and the company as a whole?
- How can I develop my potential?

A performance management process can provide a structured approach to helping individuals to address these questions.

It is vital that objectives and targets directly relate to the mission and goals of the company so that individuals understand the overall purpose of their work. This is particularly important when decisions have to be made quickly in response to customers' requirements without recourse to a manager.

A good performance management process should create a positive climate for motivation by focusing on training and development needs and by planning how these needs will be met. The competency framework should be used for agreeing targets and for creating development plans.

The challenge of responding more effectively to customers and of working in a more empowered way is not always immediately welcomed by people who have a well-established routine, previously endorsed by the management team. In BAA plc, it was found that the new way of working can raise fears of failure and lack of self-confidence in being able to master new skills. Managers must make time to work through this with each individual in a performance management process which encourages open and honest dialogue, and which emphasises the commitment of the manager and the organisation to support the individual to succeed.

MEASURING PERFORMANCE

As with any process, unless the output is measured it is difficult to assess the impact of changes and equally difficult to know how to make improvements.

Ultimately the success of the training strategy will be judged by its ability to contribute towards improved business results. BAA plc is, however, using other measures to assess success, including employee satisfaction, motivation and competence, productivity improvement and availability of suitable staff to fill job vacancies. These are being measured principally through BAA plc's performance management systems and staff surveys.

For any organization the key to sustainable success is through achieving high levels of employee performance. It is therefore vital that training strategies are truly aligned with the needs of the business concerned.

COMMUNICATION

Building Block 4 is about four things; leadership, empowerment, training and communication, and it is this fourth element that must run through the first three and can make the difference between success and failure.

Successful communication is a key ingredient at every step along the road to transforming a business at all levels, and at every location, into one that is truly committed to adopting a customer focused approach. Implementation of a new strategy will be harder and take longer without excellent communication; there can never be enough of it. If people do not understand the reasons for change, or are unclear about the methods, then, being individuals, they will each imagine something different. This will result in, at best, confusion and, at worst, conflicting effort. The skill of a good manager is in making their message relevant, and delivering it with openness and clarity.

Communication can be verbal, visual or written; the skill is to make it appropriate, to understand what it is you want to communicate and to whom, and then to select the most appropriate means. Communication can easily become a one-way street directed at staff. Equal emphasis needs to be placed on the reverse flow because, after all, it is those in an organization who are at the work-face and who have invaluable customer and process knowledge who can help a management team to focus its efforts to maximum effect.

There are many similarities between hotels and other forms of property; the only difference is that hotels let space by the day and office blocks are usually let by the year. The customer focused approach and commitment to good communication seen in the hotel industry is therefore entirely relevant to the management of property. An example is the Ritz–Carlton hotel group, a company that understands the power of communication. In addition to its group and local mission statements, the company has clearly defined a corporate culture which is communicated by means of a credo, a motto, 'three steps of service' and 20 golden rules or 'basics' which are applicable to all employees. These are printed on a pocket sized card which all employees are encouraged to carry.

The credo states:

The Ritz–Carlton Hotel is a place where the genuine care and comfort of our guests is our highest mission. We pledge to provide the finest personal service and facilities for our guests who will always enjoy a warm, relaxed yet refined ambience. The Ritz–Carlton experience enlivens the senses, instills well being and fulfils even the unexpressed wishes and needs of our guests.

The motto states:

We are ladies and gentlemen serving ladies and gentlemen.

The three steps of service are:

A warm and sincere greeting. Use the guest name, if and when possible
Anticipation and compliance with guest needs
Fond farewell. Give them a warm goodbye and use their names if and when possible

The basics include:

The credo will be known, owned and energized by all employees.
Practice teamwork and lateral service (helping each other) to create a positive work environment.
The three steps of service shall be practised by all employees.
All employees will successfully complete training certification to ensure they understand how to perform to the Ritz–Carlton standards in their position.
Each employee will understand their work area and hotel goals as established in each strategic plan.
Any employee who receives a customer complaint owns the complaint.
Guest incident action forms are used to record and communicate every incident of guest dissatisfaction. Every employee is empowered to resolve the problem and to prevent a repeat occurrence.
Uncompromising levels of cleanliness are the responsibility of every employee.
Smile – we are on stage. Always maintain positive eye contact. Use the proper vocabulary with our guests.
Be an ambassador of your hotel in and outside of the work place. Always talk positively. No negative comments.
Use proper telephone etiquette. Answer within three rings and with a smile. When necessary, ask the caller: 'May I place you on hold?' Do not screen calls. Eliminate call transfers when possible.
Take pride and care in your personal appearance.
Protecting the assets of the Ritz–Carlton Hotel is the responsibility of every employee.[10]   (Berry, *On Great Service*, 1995)

Most property managers would feel discomfort in adopting the Ritz–Carlton credo, motto and basics, but why? Customers of hotels pay for space, so do tenants of other property, so why should these longer-term occupiers of space be treated differently?

Ritz–Carlton has communicated to each and every employee absolute clarity about how their job should be done. The spirit of common endeavour that this engenders in a business is a powerful force that can help deliver corporate financial objectives. At Ritz–Carlton, communication and learning go hand in hand. On their first day employees are put through a training programme focused purely on the company culture and its values. They then go on to receive 30 days of training specific to their job.

All this is supported by day-to-day working practices. For example each day a different basic is written on department notice boards and any employee who is unclear about it or how to comply with it is encouraged to discuss it with their manager. This reinforces the corporate values and supports implementation.

Internally each hotel produces a monthly newsletter which covers local issues and is circulated to all employees at the hotel. The company also produces a quarterly magazine which is sent to all employees within the group and covers strategy, people, performance, service, human resources and global events.

Everyone employed by Ritz–Carlton understands the culture of the organization, its goals and the part they play in achieving them. They are encouraged to challenge the basics and managers work with their staff to explain how these standards can be applied.

In any business, however, a well-trained and empowered workforce cannot in isolation guarantee business success. Success comes by combining good people with good processes. Try to make good staff operate bad processes and the processes will win every time, but add good leadership, empowerment, learning and communication into the equation and the outcome should be excellent processes which deliver customer satisfaction on the one hand and shareholder value on the other.

Notes

1. Binney, G. and C. Williams (1995) *Leaning into the Future* (London: Nicholas Brealey Publishing).
2. Ibid.
3. *Motivation and Empowerment* (TQM International Ltd, 1996).
4. Sir John Egan, Chief Executive, BAA plc (1996), Freedom to Manage 'Empowerment' Booklet, p. 1 (BAA plc).
5. *Motivation and Empowerment* (TQM International Ltd, 1996).
6. Berry, L.L. (1995) *On Great Service: A Framework for Action* (New York: The Free Press).
7. Sir John Egan, Chief Executive, BAA plc (1996), Freedom to Manage 'Empowerment' Booklet, p. 1 (BAA plc).
8. Royal Society of Arts (RSA) Inquiry (1995) *Tomorrow's Company: The Role of Business in a Changing World* (Aldershot: Gower).
9. Paul Le Marquand, Assistant Group Property Director, BAA plc. Internal memorandum, 1996.
10. Berry, L.L. (1995) *On Great Service: A Framework for Action* (New York: The Free Press).

6 Process Improvement

Before considering Building Block 5, process improvement, let us take stock. By this stage a property owner knows who its customers are and what they want; it has developed a mission statement, so that it knows where the business wants to be; and it has well-trained, empowered and motivated staff capable of delivering the business goals.

A commitment to service and people willing to try to deliver that service is only half of a winning formula: none of this good work can be used to best effect if the business does not put as much time and effort into ensuring that its processes are also contributing to the business goals. Streamlined processes that are efficient, fast and cost-effective are needed to provide excellent service to the customer and, just as important, to satisfy the shareholder through optimizing productivity.

Every business is made up of a series of processes such as research and development, production, marketing, delivery and after-sales service. In addition, there are usually internal and external support processes. However, processes tend to evolve and normally over time they do not become more efficient, if anything they become less so. Often employees lack an understanding of the whole process, concentrating only on their part of the activity. This can mean that changes in the process made in isolation by one member of staff can result in severe disruption to the process at the next stage.

It seems part of human nature to add complexity to a process over time by increasing control mechanisms which with hindsight may have no good reason to be there. A further problem is that unless positive action is taken to review processes, then no advantage may be taken of technical innovations that can improve efficiency and cost-effectiveness.

The objective is to achieve improvements in the performance of processes in a business by improving efficiency, reducing costs and improving service. The aim must be to ensure that every process has the minimum number of steps, compatible with the boundaries set for the empowered staff, and that through the support of information technology (IT) each step takes the minimum amount of time.

CONTINUOUS IMPROVEMENT

Reviewing a process just once leads to an improvement, just once. With the world becoming more competitive and technical innovation developing at a rapid pace, processes need to be reviewed on a regular basis if a company is to have any chance of staying ahead.

BAA plc and other organizations have embraced the philosophy of continuous improvement as a means of driving a business forward by providing constantly-improving benefits to the customer, its employees, and the shareholders. The business benefits accrue through improvements in quality, cost and service.

Continuous improvement is a commonsense approach, described as:

> a process of continually improving the way in which we conduct our business. The process calls for clear and imaginative thinking to find better ways of doing things; ways which will improve productivity and increase levels of customer service.[1]
> (Sir John Egan, Chief Executive, BAA plc, Handbook on Continuous Improvement – Plan 1991, p. 1)

In summary, continuous improvement is:

- A management philosophy which is customer focused and believes that there is always room for improvement.
- A way of looking at business which starts from the concept that a business is made up of a large number of cross-functional and interrelated processes and tasks – these add value to resources and transform them into services which are needed to satisfy customer expectations.
- A set of tools and techniques, all of which are designed to help with the understanding and improvement of the business processes. They enable decisions to be based on facts and objective information.
- A way of managing which acknowledges that teams are more effective than individuals and that those who work at the sharp end of business are best placed to know how things can be run better.

PROCESS MAPPING

The success of any business depends on how well people design, operate and continuously improve the organization's business processes. Figure 6.1[2]

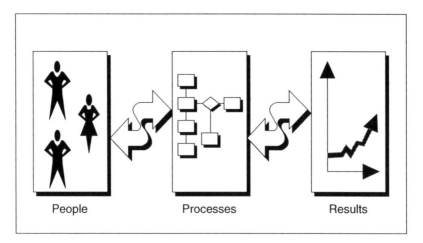

Figure 6.1   A simple model for organizational excellence (Source: TQM International Ltd, 1995)

shows a simple model for organizational excellence. Skilled people and efficient processes ensure competitiveness and lead to good financial results.

In using continuous improvement to improve processes, it is first necessary to understand the various processes that are in place by mapping them. Historically, most organizations have developed along functional and hierarchical lines and with this structure most processes have evolved, piecemeal, over time.

Figure 6.2 shows a simplified functional view of an organization, in this case an airport terminal. Each function is in a separate silo although processes often run across each one of these divisions. Figure 6.3 shows how processes cross functional boundaries. It is easy to see how processes can become inefficient over time resulting in increasing costs, lower customer-satisfaction levels and reduced competitiveness.

Key processes fall generically into two groups:

1. *Customer processes*   These deliver products and services to customers and are therefore highly visible to them. These processes are likely to generate cost and revenue and will be critically important to the business.
2. *Management and support processes*   These create and maintain the essential capabilities to run a business successfully. They will be triggered by customer processes, will usually be internal and will be separately manageable.

The business of almost any company may be broken down into a series of key stages and each stage will involve a number of processes, both customer

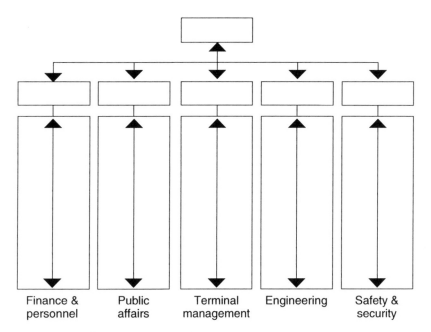

Figure 6.2   A functional view of an organization

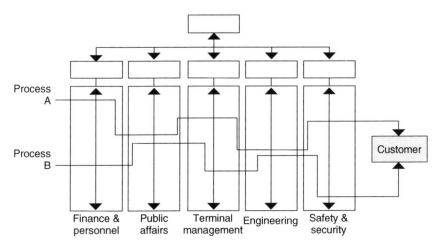

Figure 6.3   A process view of an organization

and support processes. The property business is no different and Figure 6.4 shows the way that BAA plc analyzed property customer process categories.

After having understood these customer-facing process categories, BAA plc's next step was to identify the processes within the categories shown in Figure 6.4 and to add the support processes. It was important at this point to identify, understand and map all the processes so that there were no forgotten links that could weaken the drive for improvement. There will be variations for each company but the BAA plc property process tree is shown in Figure 6.5.

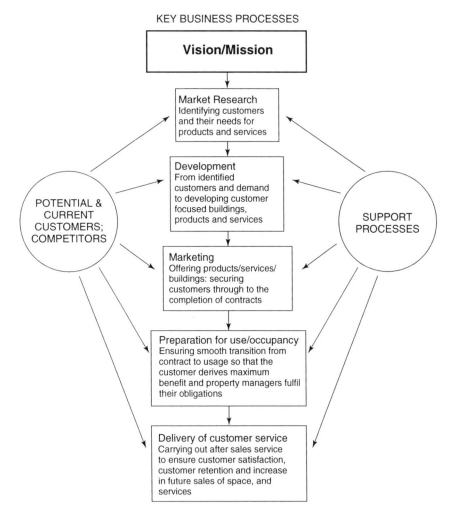

Figure 6.4   BAA plc's property process categories

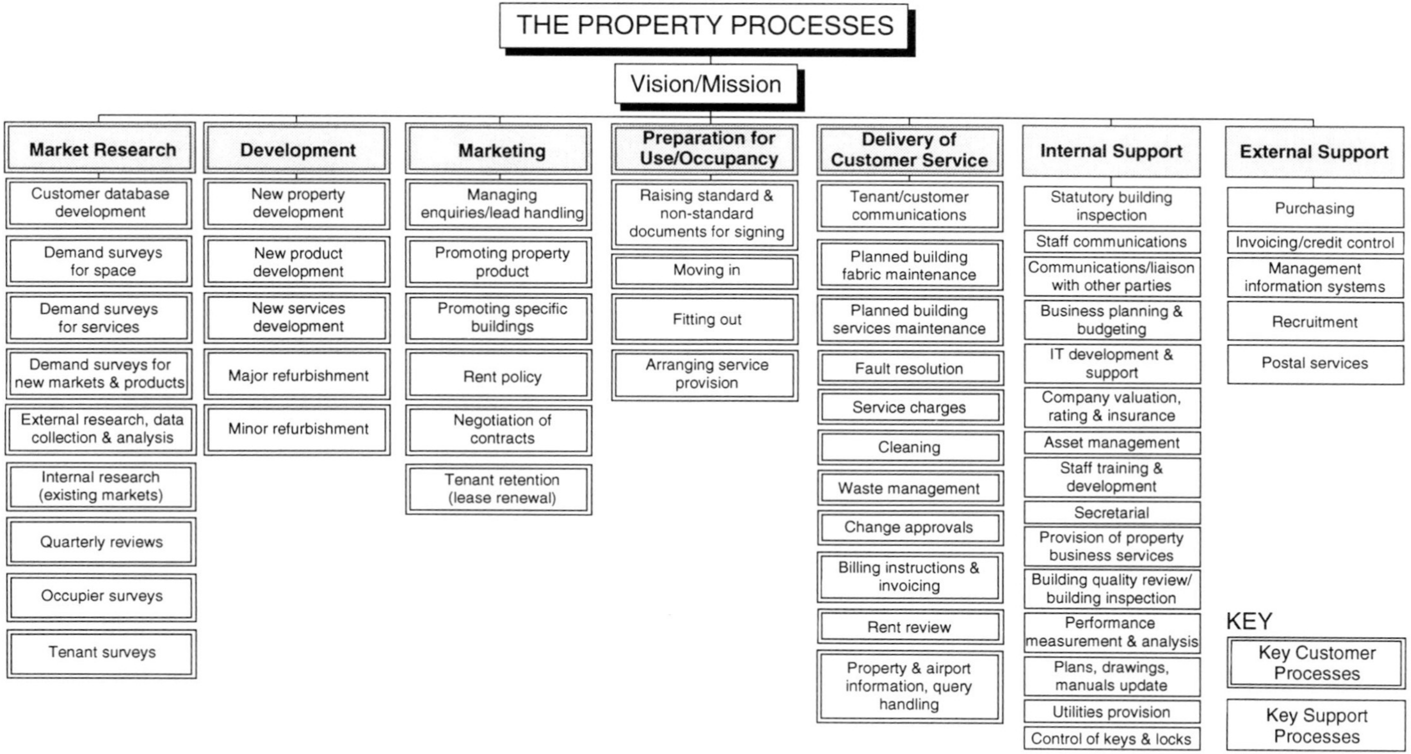

Figure 6.5 *BAA plc's property process tree*

Process problems

MARKETING   DESIGN   PLANNING   OPERATIONS DISTRIBUTION   CUSTOMER

Figure 6.6   Common problems with processes

Figure 6.6 illustrates the barriers that exist in most businesses that deliver a product or service. The process, starting with marketing and ending with the customer, should operate as effectively as a well-run factory production line. In the case of business processes a number of common problems can occur:

- Processes involve many hand-overs between people or departments, resulting in various interfaces at which things can go wrong.
- Few people, if any, understand how the whole process works – there is nobody who optimizes the process.
- Process performance is often measured inadequately or inappropriately.
- Functions or departments may optimize their part of the process, at the expense of the overall process.
- People working within a process cannot contribute fully to improvement as they may not realise the full impact of their actions.
- There is often duplication of work at each stage of the process.
- There are usually too many checks and signatures at each stage.

Tenants are naturally disinterested in how well one department operates – what they are looking for is a seamless service, and this will be achieved as a result of an efficient dovetailed process that runs across the organization.

Why improve processes?

Successful process improvement ensures that every step is necessary by eliminating any which add nothing, and that each step is as efficient as possible.
   The main benefits of process improvement are:

- reduced bureaucracy, by removing steps in the process;
- faster responsiveness, by leaving decision-making at the right (that is, lower) level and as early in the process as possible;
- more-effective use of staff time;
- cost savings;
- the ability to define performance measures;
- ensuring consistent service delivery to the customer;

- the ability of a streamlined process to take on additional workflow without compromising standards; and
- a simplified process is less likely to go wrong.

What does a good process look like? It is one that is:

- Customer focused
- Adds value and not cost
- Is clearly owned
- Is understood by those who operate it
- Is well measured
- Is continuously improved

Well-trained and motivated people operating efficient processes that deliver excellent levels of customer service should result in a competitive and therefore profitable business enterprise. Improving the process continually is what the philosophy of continuous improvement is about.

CONTINUOUS PROCESS IMPROVEMENT

At this point an organization will understand the reasons for continuous improvement, will have mapped the processes and will understand the reasons for process problems and their improvement. The next stage is to start improving each process and this can appear a daunting task and needs to be expanded in a step-by-step way. There may be no quick wins, but there will be no wins at all unless a determined long-term commitment is made to methodically improve all processes to streamline the organization. The tool for achieving this is continuous improvement.

Diagnostic steps

The first objective is to go through four diagnostic steps to prioritize the processes that need improvement:

- *Step 1 Identify activities*   Using the process tree, ask questions such as, what services are provided and why, who are the suppliers and what would be the consequences if a particular activity did not happen?
- *Step 2 Establishing the costs*   Costs need to be assigned to each process. The objective is to make an estimate of the different activity costs as a basis for decision-making.
- *Step 3 Assign a benefit to each activity*   The idea is to make an estimate of the relative rather than absolute benefits of the activities. The mission will assist in identifying which activities contribute to the organization's objectives.

- *Step 4 Prioritize by understanding the cost/benefit*   In order to help prioritize action areas, it is helpful to illustrate information on costs and benefits on a diagram. Those activities with high benefits and high costs will then be the first to undergo process improvement.

Having completed the diagnostic steps, continuous improvement methodology can be used to improve the processes in the agreed order of priority. This involves seven steps as shown in Figure 6.7.

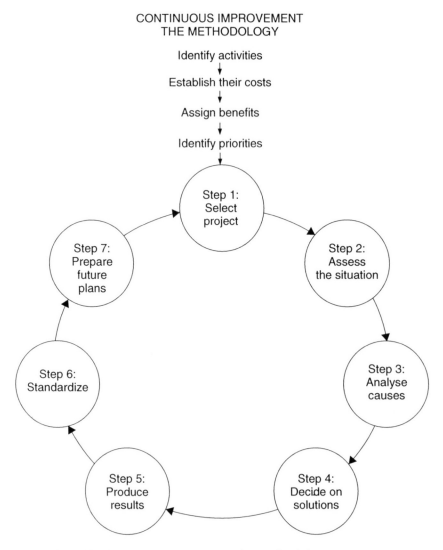

Figure 6.7   Continuous improvement – the methodology

Continuous improvement steps

- *Step 1 Select project* The diagnosis will have selected the first project and the reasons for it but where the process begins and ends need to be defined. At this stage it is also necessary to establish the boundaries of the process. For example, is the whole process under review or just part of it? At this stage targets and objectives should be set.
- *Step 2 Assess the situation* This step is concerned with gathering information about customer needs and expectations, the flow of the existing process and data which allows further understanding of the process. This detailed 'audit' is at the heart of continuous improvement and it helps to overcome the tendency to jump straight from a problem to a solution too early.
- *Step 3 Analyze causes* Now that the relevant information has been collected it should be possible to identify the root causes of a particular problem and to ask questions such as why are tenant complaints increasing or why is invoicing taking longer?
- *Step 4 Decide on solutions* Time has been spent on analyzing and understanding the activity selected without jumping prematurely into discussions about possible solutions. It is time now, in a systematic way, to generate, evaluate and select options which may solve the problems. Brainstorming sessions can help to produce a range of options. The options then need to be evaluated using criteria such as cost, resources and timescale. The solution options can then be matched against the criteria and decisions made. It is helpful to pilot a new initiative to ensure the experiment works to maximum effect, before it is given a full launch. Implementation planning and preparation to roll out the new process should be tacked at this stage.
- *Step 5 Produce results* At this stage, the objective is to ensure that the solutions or process improvements are implemented well to meet most customer requirements. To ensure the improvement is not just a flash in the pan and is sustained, customer satisfaction must be measured. A review timetable should also be put into place.
- *Step 6 Standardize* As soon as the improvement is measured to be a success it should be rolled out to all locations to ensure consistency of approach. Communication of 'success stories' is important.
- *Step 7 Prepare future plans* To remain competitive it would be a mistake to stop improvement efforts at this point. Competitors are improving, customers' requirements are changing and becoming more demanding and technology is developing. The process of improvement needs to go on. Continuous improvement means continuous improvement; it is a never-ending process as the circular model in Figure 6.7 demonstrates.

The purpose at each step of the process is to add value and if at any point this is not being achieved then different solutions need to be considered. Understanding whether value is being added requires measurement so that there is always an appreciation of what is happening and why. Actions will then be founded soundly on facts.

CASE STUDY

BAA realized as a result of tenant research that tenants at Heathrow Airport were not satisfied with the amount of time it was taking to gain landlord approval for them to carry out works. Tenants understood that special care had to be taken in an airport environment to consider issues such as operational flexibility, safety and security but they were still dissatisfied.

"*PROCESS IMPROVEMENT*"

A Change Approvals team[3] (*TQM International Ltd Newsletter*, 1994) was established to find solutions and its first step was to set team targets:

- Analyze and re-design the process and draw up an implementation plan within six dedicated days over six weeks
- Customers should have minimum involvement in the new process
- The improved process should reduce Heathrow staff time by 50%
- The new system should be capable of standardization across BAA's airports

- To provide tenants with improved information at the start of the change approvals process
- To be able to give approval within 10 working days

The old process was mapped out and measured and it was found that over many years it had grown like Topsy to become so convoluted and complex that it contained no less that 38 steps. The average time it took to give a 'yes' to a tenant was 48 days and the longest 175 days, with an exceptional best of 6 days. Improvements obviously needed to take place and a target of 10 days for all approvals looked daunting but possible.

The continuous improvement model was applied to the process, first with the appointment of a process champion who put in place a process team selected from those involved with change approvals, including a property manager, an engineer, a health and safety representative and a fire prevention officer. A 'naive resource', someone who knew nothing about the existing process, was also part of the team; their role was to challenge the norm, ensuring the team was not tempted to slip back into doing things the way they had always been done. The team was guided by the wish to improve customer satisfaction and cost-effectiveness whilst giving tenants predictability, responsiveness and flexibility.

By mapping the process the team gained a clear understanding of the flow of activities and identified a number of specific problems such as a lack of consistency across the department and major information gaps which delayed the process.

The team also identified that for any one request, property managers would have to go back to the customer at least three times for more information. At times the information could be very technical and often neither the customer nor the property manager really understood what was required. This resulted in a constant toing and froing between customer, property manager and other Heathrow departments responsible for safety, security and engineering.

The team gathered historic data to quantify the performance of the process. In addition, tenants and approval bodies such as the fire service were interviewed to identify the difficulties they faced when asked to comment on a customer request.

The data dispelled the myth that it was other Heathrow departments and approval bodies that were holding up the process. On average, half the process time was spent within the property department, at worst 70%. Most of this delay was due to bureaucracy such as counter-signing and checking of letters, which just sat in in-trays waiting for the next step in the process.

Learning from all the research and analysis and using the information gathered from speaking to the tenants and approval bodies, the team listed the value-adding steps required to meet the tenants' needs. Existing steps that were not necessary and which did not add value were cut out in the design of the now streamlined 10-step process. A 'failure prevention analysis' was also carried out to ensure the new process would run smoothly. This involved scoring the probability and consequence of any obstacles which might cause the new process to fail and actions were developed to overcome them.

The improvement was achieved by removing unnecessary approvals, but also by training and empowering front-line staff to make decisions and putting in place one-day service level agreements with other departments covering issues such as safety and security. All standard letters were put on the network system, and a simple reply form with tick boxes was designed for approval bodies to reduce the amount of time spent producing letters.

A tenant information brochure was produced describing the information required to ensure a fast response. This included the number and type of drawings required, a description of works, site inspection arrangements, contractor's safety arrangements, reinstatement policy and fire safety guidelines. A trial of the new process in Terminal 3 helped to demonstrate to staff that it was possible to turn around approvals within the 10-day timescale and identified improvements to the draft tenant information brochure prior to rolling the process out across Heathrow.

As part of the new process, team members attend 'approvals clinics' held every month at Heathrow. Tenants are encouraged to attend and discuss any work proposals in principle before submitting a request. This saves time in the long run and it is often possible to say 'yes' there and then for smaller works.

From the start the new process has been monitored continually to ensure that any problems which may occur can be highlighted and resolved quickly. The end result has been a much simplified and cheaper process that delivered all the team's targets and most importantly is delivering a fast, safe and predictable service to tenants. In order to underline commitment, BAA then gave a guarantee to tenants at all its airports:

> We will deal with 95% of all applications for approvals within 10 working days upon receipt of full information.

The commitment was backed up by a financial guarantee that in the event of failure, the next rent review would be deferred by six months.

MAKING CONTINUOUS PROCESS IMPROVEMENT WORK

Good leadership and communication are vital to the success of a process improvement programme. People will need to commit off-line time, so it is essential to win the hearts and minds of staff through effective leadership and a common vision.

The process champion should be a trained facilitator who is able to help the team map the process, and to come up with their own ideas about how the process can be improved by taking out steps which add no value.

Before the review begins, relative timescales need to be agreed by the team and days set aside for workshop sessions. Tough targets and the boundaries of the review must also be set. The people involved in a process must be the people who develop improvements and it is sensible to test solutions. The improvements in terms of better service and reduced cost should be measured and celebrated. This will, in turn, help to provide the momentum for future continuous process improvement by assisting staff to believe in their ability to find solutions and deliver benefits to customers, fellow staff and the business.

THE RESULTS

Improving processes, particularly those that have not been reviewed for years, can produce significant improvements in performance. Such change does not come without risks but if the process of change is managed in a considered way then the rewards should more than balance the risks. Figure 6.8 illustrates how standardization and incremental improvement of

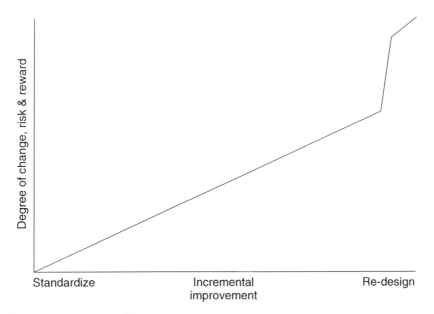

Figure 6.8   Levels of improvement

processes enhance performance but it is with the re-design of processes that the step change takes place.

Perception of value for money

A landlord that gives good value as well as good service will have higher tenant retention rates than one that does not. How is value judged? At first glance it is simple; value is assessed against the costs charged by a competitor, but if these are also viewed as being too high then that comparison will not instill a feeling of good value.

From the tenant's point of view, good value is probably achieved when property costs are at a level the business can comfortably afford. However, this perspective is one-dimensional and ignores the use of market forces to set rents. The element that is often forgotten is perception or perceived value. If someone perceives, irrespective of the actual cost, that they are receiving good value, then they are. The improvement of processes can assist in improving the perception of value for money.

The property team at Gatwick Airport devised a model (Figure 6.9) which seeks to show how to increase the perception of value for money, by balancing the need to improve the perception of quality of service and the perception of cost.

DISRUPTIVE PROCESSES

If a tenant is able to occupy space without disruption, trouble-free in every respect, then perceived value for money will increase. The right-hand side of the model, quality of service, challenges us to think of ways of reducing the disruption experienced by customers and their businesses and gives examples of such events.

The model suggests four ways of improving the process to minimize loss of perceived value through disruption:

Elimination

This eliminates the disruption by troubleshooting the root cause so that it does not recur. Costs are obviously saved as many companies have found out.

> Xerox Corporation, amongst others, has demonstrated that a company-wide improvement process can halve the cost of quality over a period of three to five years. In any business, halving costs of quality significantly improves financial performance.[4]   (C. Jones, *Management Services*, 1994)

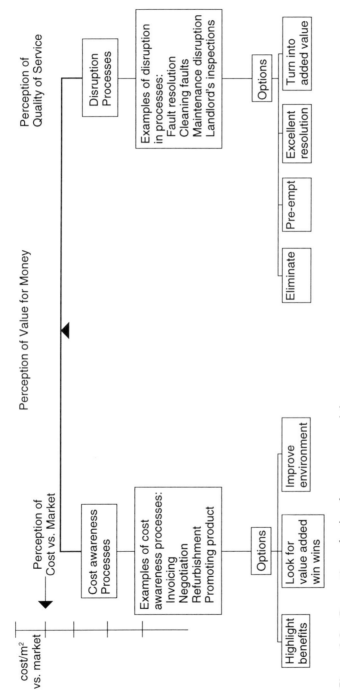

Figure 6.9 Perception of value for money model

Pre-emption

This is spotting the fault before the customer does. It is about staff and supplier involvement and co-operation. If an office cleaner, working before dawn, spots and reports a leaking tap to a landlord's engineer, the problem can be fixed before the tenant arrives at work. Other industries use pre-emption to improve customer service and therefore the perception of value for money.

> Through the application of artificial intelligence we are able, at Digital, to monitor our customers' computer systems remotely and sense up-coming problems. This allows us to anticipate problems before they even happen. For Digital, service excellence is all about anticipating needs and providing service that our customer does not yet realise that he or she wants![5]
>
> (Chris Conway, Chief Executive, Digital Equipment Co. Ltd)

Excellent resolution

This is about making it easy for a customer to report a fault and ensuring a fast and effective resolution. This requires a 24-hour fault centre, the cost of which is offset by the improved productivity provided by the slicker response and by the improved revenues through greater customer satisfaction.

Many businesses have established 0800 telephone numbers so that customers can report problems easily and at the company's expense. American Express has installed such lines and knows that it achieves responses more quickly and at 10% to 20% of the cost of handling correspondence (Cram, *The Power of Relationship Marketing*, 1994).[6]

General Electric of the USA has gone one step further by providing a centralized, expert, round-the-clock, general support service. Anyone who just has a query, not necessarily a complaint, about one of its products may call free of charge. This has greatly improved customer satisfaction.

Turning disruption into added value

Turning a disruption into a value-added service has the potential to reduce costs, as was recently experienced at Gatwick. A cleaning contractor was invited to introduce a service target to clean up accidental spillages, in addition to the planned cleaning of common areas. The contractor agreed to a one-hour response. To make it easier for customers to report accidents, and to help the cleaning contractor achieve the response target, the airport engineering fault centre was used; the process for reacting to the report being exactly the same as for an engineering fault in a baggage handling system.

Customers appreciate the one-hour clean up, so much so that the contractor is growing its business as more and more customers use it for cleaning the areas for which they are responsible. Because the contractor uses the airport's fault centre to provide this service it has agreed to reduce Gatwick's own cleaning costs on the back of the extra business generated.

So it is possible to kill two birds with one stone. Gatwick has improved the cleaning service, and hence the customer's perception of the product's value for money, and reduced the overall cost of providing the service. Turning disruption into added value is also a means of continuing to develop a competitive advantage, whilst continuing to reduce overall costs.

COST AWARENESS

Customers are aware of their costs of occupation. Focusing on quality of service is only half the story. Improving value for money also means addressing those processes that remind the customer of the charges they pay for accommodation. To be successful the business needs to focus on both sides of the model's seesaw (Figure 6.9).

The left-hand side of the model shown in Figure 6.9 asks us to think of ways to improve the perception of the charges customers pay and, as with the right-hand side, suggests some options for addressing the issues.

There are a number of options for improving value awareness such as more transparent invoicing, a customer friendly negotiation process and refurbishment to improve the physical appearance of space. Benefits can also be highlighted by promotion and branding to engender a feeling of pride in a building.

In the search for value-added gains the model can be used to help highlight customer benefits and introduce services or products that add more value to the customer's business than they cost to provide, perhaps in the environmental area. These gains benefit the customer, the supplier and the landlord, so everybody wins, thereby cementing improved partnerships and business relationships.

COMMUNICATION

Continuous process improvement is first and foremost about making real changes for the better, but perception should not be ignored. One of the keys to changing perception is to ensure the constant reinforcement of positive messages over a long period.

The property industry has considerable negative historical baggage and it will therefore take time and effort to make its customers regard it in the same light as famed customer service companies in other industries such as Avis, British Airways plc (BA) and Federal Express.

Notes

1. Sir John Egan, Chief Executive, BAA plc (1991) Handbook on Continuous Improvement – Plan 1991, p. 1 (BAA plc).
2. *What is Self-Assessment?* (TQM International Ltd, 1995).
3. Summarized from 'Process Improvement Takes Off' (Issue 11, *TQM International Ltd Newsletter*, 'Talking Quality', October 1994).
4. Jones, C. (1994) 'Adding Value or Adding Cost', *Management Services*, March, p. 20.
5. Chris Conway, Chief Executive, Digital Equipment Co. Ltd, UK.
6. Cram, T. (1994) *The Power of Relationship Marketing* (London: Pitman).

7 Information Management and Benchmarking

INFORMATION MANAGEMENT (IM)

The customer focused approach to property management described so far has covered three broad themes: mission, people and processes.

The mission gives clarity and direction and ensures that an organization's philosophy will be consistent throughout the organization and consistent over time. Well-trained and motivated people, involved in helping to shape the way an organization changes, will respond in a positive and innovative way to the drivers for change. Streamlined processes, that are fast and cost-effective, provide excellent service to the customer. They also add to shareholder value through optimizing productivity.

There is one other element that is required to link people and processes together; information systems. The journey to satisfying customers requires effective people and processes, but also excellent information systems. Information is the life-blood of an organization. Managers at the nerve centre must be given the high quality information needed to make quick, well-informed decisions. This in turn ensures that responses to customers are also fast and well-informed.

An IM strategy is the template to providing the links between people and processes and if effective will also help ensure that time expired processes are eliminated and that improved processes do not revert to being inefficient again (*Property Week*, 1996)[1].

> Information management must provide accurate and timely information which allows rapid response to customers' requirements. What could be more important?[2] (Mike Lipsey, The Lipsey Company, 1997)

Building Block 5 covers processes and IM, because IM is fundamental in supporting and streamlining processes.

WHY DEVELOP AN IM STRATEGY?

Many organizations have built up information systems over time in a piecemeal fashion, often with different departments procuring their own systems in isolation from what other parts of the business may be doing. This results in islands of information (Figure 7.1) where communication between the islands is by manual means. Consequently, information gathering takes time and effort and the results are often unreliable. This will have an adverse impact on customers, staff, their managers and ultimately shareholders.

From the customers' point of view, delays and poor quality information hardly give an impression of good service and certainly damage the perception of value for money. Any temptation to move to another service provider will be increased. Delivering good service and value to customers is dependent on staff being able to give of their best. This requires good leadership, effective training and the freedom to act; it also requires the best tools to do the job.

Providing staff with the right information systems to do their work well, improves job satisfaction and gives staff the knowledge that they are adding value to the organization. Good quality information is equally important to managers to enable them to make the right decisions in a timely manner. A manager who sets achievement targets without having good information about performance will be operating in the dark. By the time information has arrived it may be too late; customers could have already decided to take their business elsewhere.

From the shareholders' point of view, value is added to their investment in a company by the management team running a quality business that out performs competitors. A company with poor information systems will get

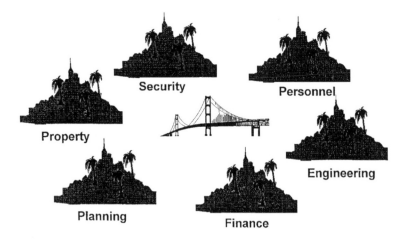

Figure 7.1   Islands of disconnected information where there is no IM strategy

by for a while but will end up being overtaken by competitors that have the systems to deliver good quality and value. In these circumstances shareholders are not known for tamely accepting second best!

Quality support systems can transform the efficiency with which a property management team operates, just as in other industries. Modus Publicity, Benetton's UK public relations agents, has states that Benetton is linked to its 80 agent offices around the world by using sophisticated IT and communication systems. The agents collect retail information from around 7000 Benetton stores across 120 countries and they place orders to the Benetton factories. Clothes are manufactured to order and can be delivered to the shops within 10 to 15 days of order (Modus Publicity).[3]

Effective use of IM is critical to a company's competitiveness in an increasingly competitive world. IM can oil the wheels of processes and help create improved processes that increase service levels and reduce costs. The introduction of a customer focused strategy that is not supported by a good IM system will result in only a fraction of the possible benefits being delivered. The aim should be not only to meet, but to exceed a customer's information requirements; anticipating them before they arise and satisfying them before the customer has fully realised that they exist.

Existing property management information technology

The evidence is that the property management software available in the market today falls short of that required by a company determined to give tenants a high level of service. Most systems are menu driven, structured databases which are not easy to use. The development of software specifically for property management has also been slower than for other management uses and little new software has appeared in the last decade.

Consequently, it has been necessary for users to accept second-best or to make bespoke alterations to standard software packages, often storing up problems for the future. BAA plc, for example, undertook a review of property management systems on the market when implementing its Property Challenge IM strategy and found nothing which met all its requirements. Accordingly BAA plc explored other systems, not traditionally seen as property management systems, and an automated workflow system based on Lotus Notes, and later called Pronto was adopted.

Jane Nelson, Property IT consultant with KPMG, highlighted software developers' slow progress towards easy-to-use systems:

> Suppliers have been reluctant to make the investment necessary in products to meet those needs.[4]   (Jane Nelson, KPMG)

She blames software developers' tendency to talk to IT departments rather that to users, resulting in emphasis on technology rather than on users' needs. It should therefore be no surprise that people often do not use the systems they are provided with, as they have not been involved in the design and specification and consequently feel that the systems are simply being imposed on them.

Nelson says that property managers compound the problem, because they are reluctant to change, even though they agree that better systems could improve decision-making. She believes the reason is inadequate training, coupled with an unwillingness to take risks. A common characteristic is that people also tend to use software for processing data and not for obtaining management information on which to base business decisions.

Property management systems must change

In addition to the earlier evidence, research points to the fact that property management systems must change. A University of Reading study examined the extent to which information on property was collected by, and was made accessible to, both property and non-property people in organizations (Avis, Gibson and Watts, *Managing Operational Property Assets*, 1989).[5] The research indicated an industry that takes too little interest in business information.

The researchers looked at companies' use of inventories (commonly referred to as 'terriers') which are little more than lists of properties. They also researched the use of property management systems which provide a great deal more information used in decision-making. The study revealed that only 70% of participating organizations claimed to have a full inventory and even worse, only 48% had partially developed a property management system.

The Reading study concluded that:

> As well as the more traditional terrier with supporting maps, plans and/or files, the property data in the organizations visited was stored in a wide variety of ways including 'in piles of files', 'on the back of fag packets', 'with the retained agent' and 'in Harry's head'.

The research identified common problems across the organizations, such as incorrect input of information and poor quality control of information entry which led to lack of confidence in the systems. In turn this led to situations where property managers had developed their own personal paper records and index lists. When stand-alone manual systems of this nature develop, an organisation is no longer in control of its information, but is reliant on a single individual or group of individuals to maintain the system. The consequence is manual systems which become non standard, resulting in the tail wagging the dog, by processes being adjusted to suit the individuals and manual systems involved. This in turn leads to low quality information, costly and time consuming information gathering and unresponsive business information support to the decision-makers.

Evidence that change is on the way

Some organizations have made the step change necessary. The Britannia Building Society has invested in IT to support a team of in-house valuers whose lives revolve around their cars, their homes and the properties they value. These 25 surveyors have no office, but have a home-based or note-book computer with a modem to communicate with their head office in Staffordshire (*Property Week*, 1996).[6] Imagine the savings in rent and petrol alone!

Northern Counties Housing Association (NCHA), one of the 10 largest in the country, found that an Enterprise information system was the answer to an information overload problem. The sudden wealth of available informa-tion created a new challenge.

> We wanted to provide access to information across the entire organization, and were determined that the system should be user-friendly enough to require minimum training of our staff. The directors realised they were embarking on a major exercise in change management.[7]
>
> (McDougall, *Executive Management*, 1995)

The system has rapidly changed the way NCHA operates by enabling users to focus on business issues rather than on the challenge of obtaining consistent information.

> We now have the tools to manage the business strategically, to enhance effi-ciency and to realign our resources in line with evolving needs. If there is such a thing as competitive advantage in a housing association, then this is it.[8]
>
> (McDougall, *Executive Management*, 1995)

WHAT EFFECTIVE IM CAN ACHIEVE

Effective IM involves the fast and accurate moving of business information around the workplace, across the business and to external parties. Moving information around the workplace – automated workflow – requires the automation of a task or process. It also involves streamlining the co-ordination and execution of that task or process. In other words, it is taking a business process from beginning to end and removing the paper involved as well as removing the time and cost taken in handling the paper. It includes electronic distribution of documents throughout the workplace to members of a team, managers and to internal and external customers.

A simple example of workflow would be the electronic distribution of a document from one person to many for approval, where only one person from the distribution list needs to approve the document, but it does not matter which one. In this example, upon approval or rejection by one person on the distribution list the document is automatically withdrawn from the others as it has now been dealt with.

Workflow can have a huge impact on the efficiency of a business. The key to the successful use of workflow systems is to automate processes that work and are well-understood. A workflow system can make a good process better and a new process possible but it can do little to improve a bad process. It is therefore essential to design improved processes, supported by, and in tandem with, the introduction of improved IM systems.

Corporations now recognize that the electronic handling of documents can greatly improve responsiveness and cost as well as requiring less storage space than is needed for a paper-based system. They increasingly realize the need to adopt a coherent strategy for managing documents with increasing emphasis on electronic formats. If documents are scanned and stored electronically they can be directed around the organization in an automated way that supports processes and can also be exchanged easily with partners and customers. Such an automated document management system gives clear gains in terms of staff productivity, time to market, efficiency and customer service.

> The main task of electronic document management is the creation, storage, maintenance, distribution and eventual destruction of documents in electronic form in order to provide improved working efficiency and support for people and organizations who need or have to rely on such documents in the course of their business.[9]   ('The Document Management Report 1995', 1995)

Many businesses enjoy the benefit of team-working and have found success is greatly facilitated by getting the IM and the IT right. The supermarket chain J. Sainsbury plc recently adopted Lotus Notes software to co-ordinate supplier and pricing information, and this has enabled it to employ smarter purchasing strategies and to obtain up-to-date supplier information. The result has been significant cost savings over a relatively short period.

IS THE INVESTMENT WORTHWHILE?

Evidence from sectors other than property show that organizations make significant returns on investment (Table 7.1) if the right IM strategy is applied. Three year return on investment for the companies in Table 7.1 ranged from 169% to 617%, demonstrating that every company received substantial financial benefits from its investment in Lotus SmartSuite and Lotus Notes. Payback periods were all less than two years and internal rates of return ranged from 34% to 264% (IDC Final Report, *Lotus SmartSuite and Notes*, 1996).[10]

Table 7.1   Organizations can make significant returns on investment in IM[11]

Company	3-year return on investment	Internal rate of return
ArboNed	411%	166%
Crum and Foster Insurance	397%	145%
Browning Ferris Industries	498%	210%
Den Kristelige Fagbevaegelse	194%	67%
Expert Database Marketing Systems, Inc	617%	264%
Philip Harmer	258%	100%
International Telecom Co.	196%	68%
MacMillan Distribution	169%	34%
Wilcoxon Construction	223%	84%

Source: IDC Final Report, p. 9.

DEVELOPING AN IM STRATEGY

The objectives when establishing an IM strategy are to ensure that it supports the business processes, is cost-effective and is a best-practice approach. It should also provide accurate real-time information and be customer focused. It follows that the system needs to be readily accessible and so must be simple and easy to use.

One of the underlying reasons for developing an IM strategy is to improve productivity and to enable users to add maximum value to their organization. This is achieved by people spending less time chasing paper and being bogged down in administrative tasks which are better handled by the system. These people can redirect their energies to the more productive area of business growth.

In developing a property IM strategy, the following steps can be taken:

- Understand the capabilities of existing IT
- Compare existing IT with best practice
- Understand business processes
- Understand the IM that is required to support business processes
- Introduce best practice IT which supports the IM strategy
- Establish a comprehensive training programme

A CASE STUDY

Set against the BAA plc property mission statement 'to fully develop our property potential and build a world-class property business... by using IT to help us deliver improved customer service…' BAA plc took the six steps to develop an IM strategy.

Understand the capabilities of existing IT

Interviews took place with business managers and key systems users. BAA plc also undertook an audit of existing systems to establish:

- the ease with which existing systems could be used at all levels of management;
- the type and accuracy of the information actually available; and
- the gap between the information required and that available.

The review found that the IT largely did what it was supposed to. However, accuracy of data was insufficient and the IT was so complicated that only a small number of expert users were able to gain access to the information held. All other managers had to rely on this small group to obtain information.

Compare existing IT with best practice

Having gained knowledge of the capabilities of the existing IT, BAA plc set about identifying the type of products which could bridge the gap between the information required and that available. This included benchmarking IM and IT solutions in the UK and in the USA to ascertain best practice. Benchmarking was also undertaken with leading UK property companies, chartered surveyors and property-owning financial institutions.

The research identified two organizations that had recognized the need to change and were taking the first steps towards a review of their IM strategy. They had identified a need for automated workflow and access to live information through user-friendly software. The benchmarking revealed that most other users were not satisfied with their IT support and the general theme was that the systems lacked responsiveness, were not user-friendly and required costly support teams to maintain them.

Understand business processes

Before considering the appropriate IT, BAA plc first had to understand business processes and how they related to each other. It was important to understand the processes first, otherwise there was the danger that the wrong IT solution could be implemented. To understand the business processes it was necessary to use a process tree (Figure 6.5, Chapter 6) as the starting point, and then to:

- align business information requirements with business processes; and
- identify the information needs of internal and external customers, business partners, suppliers and staff.

Mapping out these processes and associated information requirements produced a framework for the IM strategy which supported business objectives and ensured that all information requirements were identified and taken on board. All levels of management within the structure of the business were involved.

Understand the IM that is required to support business processes

At this point, having mapped the processes and associated information, it was possible to document the IM required to support the business processes and this became the specification for procuring the new system. It defined:

- The information requirements aligned to the business process tree
- The information requirements within the process flow charts for each of the processes in the process tree (see Figure 6.5 in Chapter 6)
- The information available from existing systems
- The method of integrating the information available from the existing systems with the new information which the new system would provide
- A common approach to efficient processes

This stage also pointed the way to introducing best-practice IT. Based on customer research an important part of BAA plc's approach was to understand changing customer requirements so that these could be accommodated. A further objective was to ensure the standardization of software to minimize maintenance costs. BAA plc obtained and documented the information through a series of structured interviews, focus groups, workshops and seminars.

Introduce best practice IT which supports the IM strategy

Having understood the capabilities of the existing IT, compared it with best practice, and determined the specification for the new IT which would support the business processes, it was time to commence procuring the appropriate IT. BAA plc adopted a low-cost, low-risk, step-by-step approach:

Prototype

A prototype was built for a small group of 10 users. Business managers and key users had specified the prototype system. Users were encouraged to experiment in a work-bench environment, exploring how business needs could be met. The prototype lasted for three months.

This experimental stage gave both the users and the IT team that would ultimately deliver the system a deeper understanding of how the IT should support the processes. The business concluded that the prototype gave it the confidence that the IM strategy was correct and with the learning and experience of the prototype behind it, the next step was to move to:

Pilot

BAA plc introduced a pilot system at Gatwick airport and two London sites and partially implemented a system at Heathrow airport. Although the prototype was a success, the step-by-step approach continued and before adopting the system across the whole of the Company, implementation across a representative part of the business was necessary. At this point, the prototype system was switched off to leave a single system.

The pilot was a success and established another milestone in achieving the customer service initiatives of the Property Challenge. When the pilot was put in place, it was found to have few software bugs and this was largely due to the learning gained during the prototype stage.

When the pilot system was fully proven the decision was taken to proceed to:

Full roll out

The system was rolled out to all locations under the banner of Pronto – standing for **PRO**perty **NeT**worked **O**rganization. Pronto focuses on the three key business areas that are important to customers; hospitality and quality, choice and value for money and it is a Lotus Notes groupware system.

Pronto comprises 27 modules (databases) as listed in Table 7.2. All 27 modules interact with each other, allowing the user to carry out a complete process, collecting relevant information from any other module. Every module is made up of standard forms which facilitate ease of use.

Table 7.2   Pronto modules

Pronto module	Description of the module
1. Actions module	Actions is a 'to do' list. It allows users to create tasks for themselves or for others. An action can be created from any part of Pronto.
2. Agreement information module	Agreement information provides, by airport, details of tenancy and lease agreements with customers, such as rents, dates and responsibilities.
3. Agreement invoices module	Agreement invoices holds details of invoice issues and provides a comparison with income due.
4. Billing instructions module	Billing instructions enables billing and tracking of income due.
5. Bug reporting module	Bug reporting allows the user to highlight any faults occurring within Pronto.
6. Change approvals tracking module	Change approval tracking manages submissions made by the customer for landlord's consent for alterations or additions to their accommodation. By using the agreement information and workflow control databases, change approval tracking is able to automatically assign and distribute information to the appropriate users for comment and approval. Any activity associated with the submission such as meeting reports, contact reports or letters can be held with the submission allowing other users to share this information to provide a seamless approach to the customer.
7. Cleaning quality monitor module	Cleaning quality monitor allows users to track cleaning quality inspections of properties within the portfolio.

Table 7.2   (Cont.)

Pronto module	Description of the module
	The reports are then held in a central database.
8. Cleaning response performance module	Cleaning response performance provides cleaning fault information allowing quick and easy access to cleaning fault data.
9. Corporate agreement information module	Corporate agreement information provides an overview of all tenancy and lease agreements across all locations.
10. Corporate property information module	Corporate property information provides an overview of the portfolio including land, building and unit information across all locations.
11. Customer contact management module	Customer contact management allows the user to create profiles on companies, business partners and people working for the companies. The user is able to track contact with a customer by creating telephone contact reports, activity reports and meeting reports.
12. Customer property (off airport) module	Customer property (off airport) holds profiles on potential 'off-airport' customer's occupations. It allows the marketing teams to track potential clients' expiries and provides marketing opportunities.
13. Faults response performance module	Faults response performance provides fault information allowing quick and easy access to fault data.
14. Health & safety initiation module	Health & safety initiation manages and tracks the issue of health & safety and fire prevention information to new occupants of accommodation.

Table 7.2 (Cont.)

Pronto module	Description of the module
15. Major development & refurbishment module	Major development & refurbishment manages and tracks larger projects.It tracks a project through all its various stages and holds information such as activity reports, business case information and correspondence relating to the project.
16. Minor projects & refurbishments module	Minor projects & refurbishments manages and tracks small projects in a similar way to the major development and refurbishment module.
17. Move out tracking module	Move out tracking manages the vacation of accommodation by customers.It triggers tasks to ensure vacation of accommodation and preparation of it for the potential customers.
18. New agreement tracking module	New agreements tracking manages and tracks new enquiries from customers as they proceed through to occupation of accommodation. Enquiries are elevated through viewing, offer, negotiation and agreement stages where a tenancy document is automatically generated based upon the terms agreed.
19. New products & services module	New products & services manages and tracks the development of new property product and service development projects.
20. Performance measurement module	Performance measurement provides a summary of all key performance measures.
21. Property information module	Property information provides, by airport, detailed portfolio information including land, building and unit information.

Table 7.2   (Cont.)

Pronto module	Description of the module
22. Property inspections module	Property inspections manages and tracks the regular property inspections undertaken. Using information held in the agreement information database it assists in the scheduling of inspections and the notification of occupants by correspondence. Property inspections allows the physical inspection reports and any activity relating to the inspection such as follow up calls and letters to be held and tracked.
23. Support files module	Support files hold scanned images, such as incoming mail.
24. Rent reviews & lease renewals module	Rent reviews and lease renewals manages and tracks rent reviews, lease renewals and amendments to agreements. It allows the user to detail the review, renewal or amendment process. The reviews will elevate through negotiation to the agreement stage where a final document can be generated based upon the new terms agreed for the customers' existing accommodation.
25. Quality of building monitor module	Quality of building monitor is a tool to manage information relating to the quality of buildings within the portfolio.
26. Waste services initiation module	Waste services initiation tracks and manages the introduction, amendment and termination of waste services provided to customers.
27. Workflow control module	Workflow control holds details on users responsible for particular tasks and assignments for each building within the property portfolio.

Establish a comprehensive training programme

New IT can be threatening for people. BAA plc's training programme had to:

- inspire confidence in the system and focus on the benefits of using the system. This required leadership from senior managers who learnt the system with all other staff and encouraged their teams to use Pronto; and
- achieve a full return on the investment in the system by ensuring it was used by everyone. Therefore the training programme had to be stimulating and enjoyable.

    Each member of staff was given one full day of basic training, followed by specific training for each group of users. For example, property managers were trained in the modules of most benefit to them whilst engineers were trained in a different set of modules. A number of business managers were trained as Pronto trainers and others as Pronto coaches. As the system went live additional training and coaching was on offer to all who required it.

The results

One of BAA plc's prime objectives was to become more responsive to customers and this has been achieved in a number of different ways, but in particular through the customer contact management module. This enables

staff to locate telephone numbers, customer details and correspondence at the click of a mouse and enables a more personal approach. The module also details the structure of companies and profiles of the people with whom business is done. Pronto has also enabled better access to information and less time is spent on administration.

The details of all aspects of development and refurbishment projects are recorded. Pronto tracks marketing enquiries, negotiations and the completion of customer agreements, monitors maintenance, and measures performance. In addition the system stores portfolio information and tenancy agreements including details of customers' other property holdings.

One of the real benefits of the new system has been faster access to information. Pronto includes a record of all incoming and outgoing correspondence. Incoming mail is scanned into the system and filed against the author. All outgoing mail is generated in the system and filed. File notes of all conversations with the companies and their employees and all actions are stored for easy access by colleagues dealing with the same customers. Any member of the team can view records relating to customers and can deal with queries and problems on the spot. Pronto produces standard letters, automatically, including a customer's name and address and other standard information. Handling correspondence automatically is another step towards the paperless office and is resulting in the removal of filing cabinets and reductions in the costs of stationery and storage space.

BAA plc is committed to property performance measurement and this is recorded in Pronto, which can measure the time taken to perform a task or the time taken to complete a process. An example of such measurement is the change approvals process, where tenant applications must be dealt with in 10 working days. All key performance measures are recorded in each module or database within Pronto with a summary view of key measures in a single module known as the performance measures dashboard module.

The Pronto project cost £1.1 million and a cost–benefit analysis has been undertaken. This can be looked at in a number of different ways:

Portfolio information	Cost of Pronto
2350 customer contacts	£468 per customer
770 810 m² lettable accommodation	£1.43 per m²
3300 agreements for occupation	£333 per agreement
Rental income (March 96) of £183.0 million	0.6% of rental income in one year

Seen from any perspective, the investment in Pronto gives good value. The cost of £468 per customer can be judged against the average annual income per customer of £78 000, not much more than two days' income. The investment has also paved the way for better customer service and has significantly improved the platform for future business growth.

A further benefit is that Pronto will release people from mundane tasks and will enable them to become involved in more productive areas of the business.

BLOCK 6   MEASURING SUCCESS AND BENCHMARKING

From courier company Federal Express to motor manufacturer Honda, companies worldwide are benchmarking in their search to become the best in their field.

Indeed, since its inception about 25 years ago, benchmarking has become one of the management tools used most widely by companies seeking to organize processes efficiently and cost-effectively and to satisfy their customers better. Simply put, benchmarking is an objective but comparative technique for the analysis of information about production or service delivery, costs, or the quality of a finished product. The comparison is with a known set of data or criteria.

Benchmarking against current best practice helps an organization to improve each element to equal, and ultimately exceed, that standard. Putting into place best practice moves a company towards being the world's best.

Technique and development

The first use of benchmarking is generally attributed to the copier company Xerox which sought to understand the drivers behind the success of Japanese competitors in the 1970s. By comparing and analyzing processes, benchmarking helped identify the competitors' advantages which had toppled Xerox from the dominant market position it had enjoyed for many years.

Given the fundamental assumption that benchmarking will lead to improvement, it follows that measurement of elements such as customer service and cost can be vital for developing a quality business. Processes also need measurement; without it there can be no understanding of where things stand and whether they are actually improving. Without measurement there is no hard information to let a manager, supplier, business partner or customer know if agreed goals have been achieved. In short, if measurement does not take place, improvements are unlikely to be made and certainly will not happen spontaneously.

Structured comparative analysis through benchmarking is not just important for companies which seek the status of world's best. Without benchmarking there can be no depth of understanding about the quality of the process or of the entire corporation, or how improvements can, and are, being made.

PROGRESS IN BENCHMARKING

Benchmarking can range from internal comparisons to global ones. As an organization develops the quality of its product or service it will seek more challenging benchmarks with the ultimate aim of being the best in the world. This works as follows:

Performance measurement

This is an accurate internal measurement of performance in areas that are important for the achievement of the company's mission. Performance measurement replaces 'I think' with 'I know'. In the case of the BAA plc Property Challenge, performance measurement of customer satisfaction is through the tenant and occupier surveys which cover issues important to customers. These surveys produce vital information on which management action should be based.

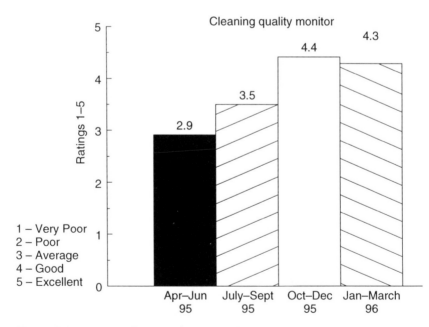

Figure 7.2   Terminal 3, Heathrow, performance measurement

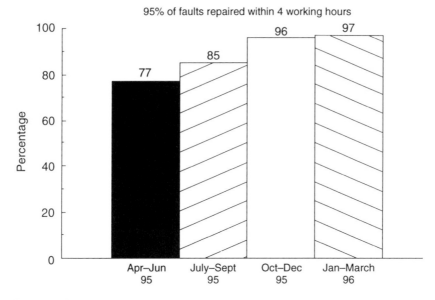

Figure 7.3   Terminal 2, Heathrow, performance measurement

As an example, in early 1995 when cleaning standards were measured at Heathrow Terminal 3, performance was not up to standard and improvements had to be made. Figure 7.2 shows the results.

A landlord's performance against goals can also be measured as in the case of the BAA plc Property Challenge promise to respond to 95% of all faults within four working hours. Figure 7.3 shows how performance improvement was measured at Heathrow Terminal 2.

Competitive benchmarking

The next, more-testing level of benchmarking for a company is to compare its performance with that of competitors. In the UK property industry this is difficult because so little measurement takes place, but property benchmarking in the USA is more developed.

Other industries are more familiar with competitive benchmarking. For example, the car-maker Rover halved the time it took to test products by benchmarking itself against Honda. Also, British Rail, prior to the privatisation of the system, benchmarked itself in its cleaning of trains against the cleaning of planes by British Airways (BA), and this helped it cut the cleaning time to eight minutes a train.

A good example of competitive benchmarking in the UK property market is Jones Lang Wootton's Office Service Charge Analysis Research, (OSCAR, 1996),[12] which compares service charges paid by occupiers of multi-let office buildings. The survey details different cost components such as insurance and air conditioning and covers buildings of varying sizes and ages in various locations.

Understanding trends through benchmarking can produce interesting results which can help focus management action. The 1996 OSCAR report showed service charge trends between 1983 and 1995. In the case of non-air conditioned buildings energy cost had increased by 7% but heating and maintenance costs by 190%. Therefore is there something that the energy companies can teach those companies who manufacture and maintain heating systems? And if the insurance industry can reduce costs over 12 years by 58.3% why has the cost of management of buildings increased by 81.8%?

Process benchmarking

This benchmarks particular processes across industries. For instance, the time to clean 100 seats in a train could be compared with how long it takes the best in the cinema industry to do the same job.

For property owners, it is always interesting and relevant to compare property management performance with that of the hotel industry. Such process benchmarking shows how improved performance is achieved and makes testing targets believable to a sometimes sceptical management team.

Strategic benchmarking

Strategic benchmarking goes beyond the comparison of company processes or operations to ask 'How do this company's long-term strategies, plans and performance compare with others?' It requires an insight into the high-level thinking of each organization. When successful it provides valuable information about judgements of the best experts in any business on the long-term trends to be addressed, and the range of responses to be applied.

Global benchmarking

Global benchmarking is the pinnacle of benchmarking methods. It widens the net of comparisons beyond direct or indirect competitors, or even national market leaders. It compares a company with the very best operations worldwide in a similar field. Thus, a domestic UK airport may compare itself with the very best domestic US airport, even though they do not compete for traffic. It may extend the comparison across industries, as well as countries to compare, say, passenger care in the UK airports with visitor care in the Pacific Rim hotels.

CONCLUSION

This chapter has considered how IM can be the essential link between people and processes. Add this to a well-trained and empowered team benchmarking its performance against world standards, and there is every prospect of delivering excellent financial performance, all the time.

Notes

1. The Builder Group, *Property Week*, 9 May 1996, p. 36.
2. Mike Lipsey, The Lipsey Company, Internal communication, January 1997.
3. Modus Publicity, 1j. Montagu Mews North, London WH1H IAJ (Miss Seema Merchant).
4. Jane Nelson, Property IT Consultant, KPMG.
5. Avis, M., V. Gibson and J. Watts (1989) *Managing Operational Property Assets*, pp. 23–31 (A Report of Research of Organisations in England and Wales) Copyright University of Reading and published by Graduates to Industry.
6. The Builder Group, *Property Week*, 28 March 1996, p. 39.
7. McDougall, A. (1995) Northern Counties Housing Association, *Executive Management*, Autumn 1995, p. 33.
8. Ibid.
9. 'The Document Management Report 1996' (Cambridge Market Intelligence), in *Corporate IT Strategy*, September 1995, pp. 28–9.
10. IDC Final Report (1996) *Lotus SmartSuite and Notes: Beyond Team Computing*, International Data Corporation, Five Speen Street, Framlingham, MA 01701 USA, p. 9.
11. Ibid.
12. OSCAR 96, *Office Service Charge Analysis Research* (Jones Lang Wootton, 1996).

8 The Partnership Approach to Value for Money

There can be few industries around the world that are not constantly striving to find ways of giving their customers value for money: property, with few exceptions, is one of them. In an increasingly competitive and over-supplied real estate market, it is the landlords that succeed in giving good value that will prosper; the others may fall by the wayside.

The property industry, like any other, can be analyzed using Michael E. Porter's theory of five competitive forces, with competing landlords all facing competition from each other, the threat of new entrants, supplier bargaining power, buyer bargaining power, and the threat of substitutes such as alternative types of accommodation (Porter, *Competitive Advantage*, 1985).[1]

One of the principal tenets of Porter's theory is that these forces threaten a sector's profitability and the profitability of individual companies within that industry. Porter analyzes the effects of these forces and the reactions of competing organizations and concludes that one response by competitors is to differentiate their products and services from those of their rivals. The purpose of differentiation is to stimulate demand for a brand, product or service and move competition away from price-driven criteria to ones of quality and customer satisfaction.

For a property owner, differentiation could take many forms, but an example might be environmental issues. In the case of environmental legislation a property owner is often in a better position than a tenant to interpret what has become a flood of new regulations. Providing tenants with an up-to-date environmental information service showing how they can cut pollution, procure from sustainable sources and reduce energy costs would be the mark of a landlord that is seeking competitive differentiation. Good management of environmental issues is also likely to cut the landlord's overall costs, as well as proving that the company takes its wider responsibilities seriously.

PRODUCT DIFFERENTIATION

For good examples of differentiation, one only has to consider the airline market which is never short of new entrants. Nevertheless, against the backdrop of increasing supply and price cutting, some airlines, such as British Airways (BA), have continued to prosper and grow. There are many reasons behind BA's success, but one of the strongest has been its emphasis on customer service which has differentiated it from its rivals. An example was BA's introduction of arrivals lounges. Research showed that business people often crossed the Atlantic overnight and then had little option but to arrive at their first meeting feeling crumpled and unrefreshed. The introduction of arrivals lounges where business passengers could shower and have breakfast, at no extra cost, gave the airline a clear competitive advantage.

BA is constantly seeking ways to differentiate it's product to ensure that the passengers' total travel experience is one that they will wish to repeat again and again. Sir Colin Marshall, the Chairman of BA, has talked about 'orchestrating service' as:

> arranging all the elements of our service so that they collectively generate a particular experience. We try to think about what kind of impression or feeling each interaction between the company and a customer will generate. For instance, we ask our crews not to load up passengers with food and drinks and then disappear – not for cost reasons but so we can create additional personal contacts with the customer. According to our research, just seeing crew members creates higher customer-satisfaction levels. Other airlines pile on the food and drinks so that their crew members don't have to go back.[2]
> (Prokesch, *Harvard Business Review*, 1995)

Could the following comment by Sir Colin Marshall be equally applicable to a customer focused property manager?

> I mentioned that we strive to make our customers' travel experience seamless, personal, and caring. We continually ask customers in focus groups to tell us what such an experience should look and feel like, and we have distilled their responses into service principles that are enshrined in two of our corporate goals. The goals are: 'To provide overall superior service and good value for money in every market segment in which we compete' and 'to excel in anticipating and quickly responding to customer needs and competitor activity'. These corporate goals have, in turn, been incorporated into our customer service department's mission statement: 'To ensure that British Airways is the customer's first choice through the delivery of an unbeatable travel experience.'[3]   (Prokesch, *Harvard Business Review*, 1995)

In Porter's theory, this product differentiation has led to BA's strength in its sector of the market based not solely on price, but on value. Value – defined as satisfaction minus price – has been increased by the high levels of satisfaction produced by the company's service strategy.

The supermarket industry is another interesting example where increasing competition has led companies to distinguish themselves by customer service initiatives; choice, free advice and customer loyalty schemes. Tesco, for example, introduced a quality guarantee on meat, bread and fresh produce, a customer-care line which resulted in no sweets at the checkouts and cheap petrol available 24 hours day. Tesco was also the first UK supermarket chain to introduce a loyalty card, and other supermarket groups have followed this lead.

What is the relevance of all this to property management? It is simple; successful landlords will differentiate themselves at least in part by improved customer service and better value for money which will create an edge over competitors. Differentiation is achieved by first gaining a clear understanding of the tenants' wishes and then finding innovative and cost-effective ways to meet or exceed those wishes. A well-defined and differentiated product, even a property one, should then be capable of being developed into a brand.

Coca-Cola has developed a brand with an excellent reputation. Is it too far fetched to imagine that a landlord could establish such an image? This could be countrywide, covering all types of property, or, less ambitiously, countrywide but restricted to a single product. For customers, a BAA plc McArthur Glen branded designer outlet centre clearly is different from traditional shops, reinforced by the knowledge that they can buy world-renowned brands at a 30% discount. Single buildings, particularly large ones, are well-placed to develop a well-defined brand image based on creative and excellent value added customer services.

In the area of serviced offices, Regus are creating an international brand similar to that of an hotel, recognisable for consistent and predictable levels of service. Typically a Regus business centre, as well as providing flexible office space, will also provide a range of support services to make the occupiers life as easy as possible. These include a personalized telephone line, individually adjustable air conditioning, free advice on telecommunication services, access to the Regus bar, accounting and legal advice and three complimentary days each month for use of an office or conference room in one of 110 centres worldwide.

> What we need is to transfer more of the best hotel service culture, reliability, consistency, responsiveness and personal attention – to the modern office environment.[4]   (Tony Edwards, *Property Week Supplement*, 1996)

Using customer-oriented property management to differentiate, switches the emphasis from what Dr Tony Alessandra (*Relationship Strategies*, 1990) calls 'conquest selling' to 'relationship selling'[5] In the case of property this means moving away from 'the deal' being the beginning and end and the only measure of success. It means adopting a philosophy where the true mark of a high-quality organisation is regarded as the successful establishment and maintenance of long-term relationships.

A property product, designed to help establish that relationship, can be differentiated in a host of different ways depending on property type, location and the product offer of competitors. Most of all, it needs to be focused on the needs of customers.

BAA plc, through the Property Challenge, has set out to differentiate the service given to tenants in a number of ways. Here are some examples:

- *Lease flexibility* Airlines are in a fast-evolving business; they are constantly forming alliances, opening up new routes and finding new ways of doing things. They require flexibility, and any airline occupying space at a BAA plc terminal can now hand back all or part of the space at three-months' notice, with no penalty.
- *Lease terms* For much of the terminal accommodation, a simple standard short-form tenancy agreement has been prepared in co-operation and agreement with the tenants' professional advisers. BAA plc took the bold step of eliminating those standard covenants on which it had never relied in the past. The result is that the agreement is predictable, enabling fast conclusion with little, if any, legal input.

- *Lease translations* The customers include many foreign companies, and the English version will be translated into the relevant language. At present, five European languages are proposed, but this is likely to increase.
- *Inclusive leases* Some tenants prefer rents to exclude rates and service costs so there is total transparency, while others prefer to know their total occupancy costs. Both these requirements are accommodated.
- *Pre-delivery check* A 'no snags' guarantee is given that all accommodation will be entirely fit for use on handover. After all, no self-respecting motor manufacturer would deliver a car without a thorough pre-delivery check and so why should the same principle not apply to property?
- *Fault resolution* A guarantee to resolve 95% of property faults, anywhere on the airport, within four working hours.
- *Approvals for tenant works* A guarantee that 95% of applications for approval of changes in a customer's accommodation will be dealt with within 10 working days of receipt of full information from the customer.
- *Cleaning standards* These, judged with the involvement of tenants, will meet agreed and improving standards.
- *Legal documentation* A guarantee in England to issue 95% of draft standard tenancy documents for terminal accommodation within five working days of detailed heads of terms being agreed.
- *Moving in* Lease signing is not an end in itself but signals the beginning of a relationship that starts with moving in, when a customer

service manager will be in attendance, an engineer on call and everything will be done to be welcoming and hospitable right down to
putting on a moving-in party and delivering welcome flowers. The
cost of these initiatives is small but the message is big: 'You are
important to us and we care about you!'

The intention of this approach is to help differentiate BAA plc as a landlord
and to help it grow its market share at a time when technology is making it
easier for companies to base their operations not just outside the airport
but, in some cases, anywhere in the world.

COMMUNICATION

If differentiation is one of the keys to competitive success, then good
two-way communication is what ensures that new products or services are
relevant and add value to the tenant's business.

An easy mistake is for a property owner to find a problem and then just
as quickly come up with a solution that it believes will satisfy the tenant;
the solution may not. An example might be fire drills which not many
occupants enjoy; they are essential, but interrupt work and take up time. A
considerate landlord might come up with the idea of giving everyone
involved in the fire drill a tube of Smarties as they are patiently waiting outside the building. This sounds like a good idea, but did anyone ask the
people working in the building? If so, perhaps the answer would have
been: 'Smarties are a kind thought but what we would really like is a simple canvas cover that stops us getting soaked in the rain while we are waiting for the building to be given the all clear'.

Good two-way communication helps ensure that management effort is
directed at achieving what the customer actually wants, as well as testing
tomorrow's ideas for differentiated products.

PRODUCT DEVELOPMENT

It is interesting to glimpse into the future and think about some of the fea-
tures that might become the norm as landlords attempt to introduce competitive products.

Service charges

Will service charges be capped so that any costs in excess of budget are
borne by the landlord? In a particularly cold spell it would be strange
indeed to be told by an hotel that there was a supplement to cover unbud-
geted fuel costs!

Most occupiers of buildings, in order to remain competitive in their own industries, must improve their productivity each year. Perhaps excellent landlords will set out to help their tenants achieve these performance improvements. One way of doing this would be to ensure that building service and maintenance costs remain constant in real terms, if not fall. This spirit of partnership would help develop a longer-term business relationship.

Service recovery

If the tenant is paying for a service which the landlord fails to deliver, will there be penalties? An hotel bathroom without hot water would result in a price reduction. Surely landlords need to develop service recovery policies where fair compensation is given in the event of service failure.

Service level agreements

Will landlords of tomorrow be prepared to accept financial responsibility for all the suppliers to a building? For instance, in the case of a multi-let building, the landlord has more buying power than any individual tenant. The landlord is well placed to enter into service level agreements with suppliers, say for the repair of telephone equipment faults within a set number of hours. This benefit, together with an appropriate financial guarantee could then be passed on to tenants.

PRODUCT DEVELOPMENT: A CASE STUDY

As part of BAA plc's Property Challenge, Gatwick Airport decided to find a way of adding value to the day-to-day lives of the 25 000 people who work for tenant companies. The result was the introduction of a personal door-to-door, office-to-office concierge service available to all property occupiers working in the various companies that operate within the airport boundary.

Gatwick has signed a partnership deal with Airport Concierge Limited which provides a dry-cleaning service, delivers office provisions from tea to washing-up liquid, organizes event tickets, prints stationery, and arranges to deliver gifts. New services and products are planned. Customers receive their personal 'Concierge Card' and PIN number and are able to place orders on a freephone service. The service is designed to offer both convenience and competitive prices with a high level of service delivery.

> In improving property services at Gatwick, we are committed to providing our customers with the highest level of property management services at prices which offer

value for money. Airport Concierge provides an additional package of benefits aimed at saving our customers time and enables them to operate their businesses more efficiently.[6]

(Jeremy Boyes, Property Director, Gatwick Airport Limited, BAA plc)

Similarly, at Heathrow Airport a privileges scheme was introduced for all airport employees. Under the scheme, credit cards were issued entitling each employee to discounts on a range of products, including currency exchange, leisure pursuits, health and fitness and discounts on travel. Discounts are also available on a range of restaurants, bars and cafés as well as at clothes, footwear and chemists shops.

Neither of these schemes would have been capable of achieving the critical mass necessary to be successful without the full involvement of BAA plc as landlord and facilitator. This is true for many property owners, whether of small or large portfolios, who have access to a business community that can provide the scale to make economies through bulk purchasing power.

Tenants often have very straightforward, commonsense demands, and the introduction of new products and services can help deliver what is required. A director of Salomon Brothers commented:

I want an owner prepared to provide service, really manage his asset for my benefit and keep me happy.[7]   (Andrew Rabeneck, *Property Week Supplement, 1996*)

The challenge for landlords is to deliver a service that meets tenants wishes.

PARTNERING

In the property industry, the concept of partnering is rare, but commonplace in other industries. An example of the approach is car manufacturer Nissan's introduction to the UK of supplier development teams who work closely with key suppliers on overall manufacturing improvement. The teams focus on issues such as production line efficiency, quality improvement, inventory reduction and aims to assist suppliers in their drive for lean manufacturing and sustainable world-class performance (CBI, Partnership Sourcing in Action, 1996).[8]

In the case of Sommer, which supplies carpets and soft interior trim for Nissan cars, the development teams significantly cut production times and introduced just-in-time deliveries every 20 minutes, reducing the stockholding costs of both companies.

Sommer has a strong innovation capability, which makes such a close and dedicated partnership possible.[9]   (Geoff Smith, UK Purchasing Manager, Nissan)

In 1993 Sommer won Nissan's award for most-improved supplier, and a year later achieved the ultimate best-supplier award. Sommer naturally welcomes and gains great benefits from the improvement to its business that has resulted from working with Nissan. The two companies, one a customer and the other a supplier, have developed a partnership approach that has benefited them both.

Compare this with the typical approach to property management through the landlord and tenant relationship which, after all, is also one between a customer and a supplier. Traditionally there is an initial contact to negotiate the terms of the lease, subsequent rent review meetings, periodic inspections to police the landlord's covenants and then negotiations to renew the lease, often undertaken by third parties representing the respective parties. The periodic arrival of legal notices throughout the lease does not help to instill the tenant with a feeling of partnership.

During the lease the landlord usually focuses very little on how to add value to the tenant's business. By showing little interest, the landlord is unable to be responsive to changing needs and so does little to encourage tenants to renew their leases. This last point is significant as the cost of marketing buildings is high and empty space means an expensive loss of income. But the traditional landlord and tenant model takes little account of this, despite the cost-effectiveness of the approach.

The landlord often has great buying power which, if it cares to use it, can be harnessed to benefit both landlord and tenant. By this partnership approach, the landlord is contributing to the financial success of the tenant and in turn can gain reward; a 'win–win' situation which has every chance of outliving and expanding beyond the parameters of the initial lease.

"THE PARTNERSHIP APPROACH"

Value-added services

One of a landlord's prime objectives should be to give tenants good value. This becomes more difficult in the case of a small single-tenanted building where it is less easy to introduce value-added services and where the rent is established by market forces. This is not the case where the landlord manages a large estate of buildings or indeed a single large building; here there are no good reasons why a landlord should not set out to give tenants value for money.

A good example of how a company can earn revenue from value-added services is Regus which has developed a worldwide business of fully serviced business centres. The percentage of the company's income from rent has been reduced to the extent that services such as faxes, photocopiers and video conferencing now make up a substantial proportion of the company's revenue.

A customer focused approach to property management will lead to better value for tenants but that does not necessarily mean at less rent. Value-for-money services will help ensure good overall value, thereby securing rental levels and giving prospects for growth in a way that does not compromize value to the occupier.

VALUE SHARING

In the field of property management, as in other industries, new services or products can be introduced that add more value to customers' businesses than they cost to provide. Because these add benefits to the customer, the supplier and the landlord, everybody wins, thereby strengthening partnerships. This whole approach differentiates market leaders from followers and although value sharing is an exciting area it is one that is neglected by the property industry.

The goal is to add value by either saving money or increasing income. This can be split into two areas, the corporate and the personal. In the first, value can be added to a company's business, thus helping to create an attractive marketing package for prospective occupiers or a reason for tenants to stay. In the second, the landlord rises to the challenging notion that every individual who occupies a building is a customer. If value can be added to people's working lives then their employers will have more incentive to stay in, or move into, the landlords property.

This approach relies on an owner's ability to use its property estate as the market and its relationships and buying power with its suppliers to provide services to that market. In facilitating access to its market, as in the case of Airport Concierge at Gatwick described earlier in this chapter, BAA plc promotes a low-cost and low-risk entry for its suppliers. This means that it will promote a supplier's product or service to its customers provided the supplier agrees to meet certain standards.

For example, the supplier provides a price guarantee at an agreed minimum percentage below its normal retail price. This ensures that BAA plc's smallest customer benefits from a lower price whilst the largest customer can negotiate volume discounts.

This low-cost and low-risk approach ensures that suppliers are willing to give the opportunity a go. There is no need to carry out expensive market research or selectively target customers; all that is required is the promotion material. From BAA plc's perspective, even if an occasional supplier initiative was unsuccessful the very fact that the offer has been organized would have helped to improve customer perception.

The provision of shared services by landlords is still embryonic but the opportunities are considerable. What will the future hold? Why would landlords of large multi-occupied buildings not have framework agreements with office equipment suppliers, fit-out contractors and maintenance firms, all working to high, guaranteed standards and with competitive costs? This will come, and when real value is being given to the tenant surely it is only a small step before a fair proportion of that value is enjoyed by the landlord.

THE RESPONSIBLE OWNER

The quality of the environment and the health, safety and security of people at work have always been important issues for owners of property but, quite rightly, society is now demanding ever-higher standards. This trend will continue as the environment changes for the worse because of the use of energy in all its forms, the production and disposal of waste, the use and wastage of natural resources and population growth.

Many tenants, particularly smaller companies, are often less well-informed than they might be about these issues, and this is an area where a forward-thinking, responsible owner, can add great value to a tenant's business. The landlord, by adopting a partnership approach, is ideally placed to help tenants achieve best practice in the areas of environment, health, safety and security.

This section is not intended to cover these issues in a comprehensive way but to act as a marker of two things. The first is that as environmental pressures grow so will society's demands on developers and owners of buildings to act in a more responsible way. The second is that the law is fast moving in a direction where owners, irrespective of the actions of tenants, suppliers and contractors, may be deemed to be responsible for lapses of safety or pollution control over land and buildings they own.

Pollution

For the property sector, the big issue is contaminated land. It has been esti-mated that up to 60% of derelict land in the UK is contaminated. Most land and waterways have been heavily polluted by industrial processes, the effects of which were either unknown or widely ignored at the time.

Anyone who caused or knowingly permitted contamination of a site can be charged for the cost of the remediation of that land. If they cannot be found, the owner or occupier will be responsible for the clean-up.

Water

The Water Resources Act 1991 made it an offence to cause or knowingly permit any poisonous, noxious or polluting matter or any solid waste matter to enter 'controlled waters' which includes all drains, surface water gullies, ditches and water in or in contact with underground strata.

Noxious chemicals and materials with the potential to cause soil, surface and ground water contamination must be stored in watertight bunded areas. Regulations cover the design of the bund area, the need for specialist licenced contractors to remove the contents and the owner's responsibility to keep accurate records.

Waste

All businesses must analyze their waste before disposal and all controlled waste must be bagged and deposited in suitable containers for collection by an authorized contractor. A compulsory transfer note is required, describing the waste accurately.

Special waste, which has the potential to harm people or the environ-ment, has to be disposed of in a licensed site by a licensed contractor. It is an offence to dump such waste, if it includes material that may contam-inate the atmosphere.

Under the Finance Act 1996, a landfill tax of £2 per tonne of inactive waste and £7 per tonne of all other waste was introduced in October 1996 on all waste deposited in landfill, in order to encourage production of less active waste and more recycling.

Energy

The use of energy to provide lighting, power, hot water and air condition-ing in buildings produces carbon dioxide and sulphur dioxide which con-tribute respectively to global warming and acid rain.

Each year in the UK in excess of £800 million worth of energy is used in building services. It is believed that this could be cut by up to 20%. A first step should be an energy audit covering costs, usage, thermal characteristics and the efficiency of plant and equipment. The building systems should then be surveyed individually.

Good practice requires lighting to be cleaned and maintained regularly to maximize the efficacy of lamps, and low-energy lamps installed. An 18W compact fluorescent lamp produces as much light as a 100W bulb. Natural light should be used as much as possible, with light sensors and timers to switch off lights automatically. People should also be encouraged to use task lighting and to switch off lights when they are not needed.

Equipment such as lifts, escalators, office machines, boilers, heaters, pumps and ventilation systems should be well maintained to maximize energy efficiency. Forced ventilation systems may need to capture and dispose of any contaminating emissions from the manufacturing processes in a building.

Air conditioning is a large contributor to a building's capital and running costs and its energy consumption. Therefore the question of whether air conditioning is needed should be asked at the building's design stage. Alternative systems, using fans and filters, can provide cooling without the expensive chillers that consume large amounts of energy and can leak CFC gases which deplete the ozone layer. If air conditioning is installed, a building management system should be used to optimize its operating efficiency. The high capital cost of a building management system is offset by future energy savings, particularly as energy availability is expected to fall and energy prices rise.

Health and safety

A building owner that controls any part of the premises is responsible for compliance with health and safety legislation. Laws covering health and safety of workers in the UK extend right back to 1802 with the Health and Morals of Apprentices Act which sought to control the working hours of apprentices in the cotton industry. The moral responsibility that a building owner shoulders, over and beyond the legal responsibility, is as relevant today as it was in 1802.

The Health and Safety at Work Act 1974 was intended to anticipate and prevent accidents through general duties that apply to any workplace. Enforcing authorities can issue improvement and prohibition notices on employers to comply with the law. Regulations and codes of practice issued under this Act have made most previous legislation obsolete.

Following European Union directives, 1992 also saw a 'six-pack' of important regulations passed in the UK: the Management of Health and Safety At Work Regulations; the Workplace (Health, Safety and Welfare) Regulations; the Provision and Use of Work Equipment Regulations; the Manual Handling Operations Regulations; the Health and Safety (Display

Screen Equipment) Regulations; and the Personal Protective Equipment at Work Regulations. These regulations are supported by Health and Safety Executive (HSE) documents, publications and codes of practice. In addition, British Standards and guidelines from industry bodies and associations are also referred to by the enforcing authorities and used as a yardstick.

In property management, much of the legislation and recommendations contribute towards good management and added value through energy saving. The goodwill between the customer and the services provider is enhanced when the customer feels that they have been provided with good value as well as a safe working environment.

Building services

Most plant and machinery that supply services to premises are subject to statutory inspection. The Offices, Shops and Railways Premises (Hoists and Lifts) Regulations 1968 require lifts and hoists to be of good mechanical construction and properly maintained. An examination is required every six months and an industry guideline calls for inspections and checks to different parts of the system over cyclical 10-year periods. Certificates and records must be kept for inspection.

The Electricity at Work Regulations 1989 apply to a wide range of plant, systems and work activities and to electrical systems at all voltages. The Institution of Electrical Engineers recommends an annual visual inspection of electrical systems and a full inspection and test at intervals of no more than five years.

Fire safety

There is a string of legislation covering fire safety. Workplaces with more than 20 employees, or with more than 10 working other than on the ground floor, require a fire certificate from the local fire authority for occupation of the premises for the purposes of carrying out a business. There may be an exemption if the authority is satisfied that the fire risk to occupants is not serious.

A fire certificate states the means of escape, the method of escape, the fire warning system, and the fire fighting system. Maintenance and regular testing of all equipment, and annual evacuation drills, are also required. Failure to comply can result in an improvement notice being served on the duty holder or, in an extreme case, a prohibition notice which bans the use of the premises until the fire authority is satisfied that there is no longer any danger to the occupants.

Hazardous substances and biological agents

The Control of Substances Hazardous to Health Regulations 1994 is intended to prevent workplace illness and/or disease from exposure to hazardous substances. An adequate assessment of the risks from work activities must be carried out and control measures and monitoring introduced.

One of the most important concerns for property managers is the possibility of *Legionella* bacteria multiplying in heating, hot and cold water and air conditioning systems and causing legionnaires' disease.

Another concern is sick-building syndrome which is believed to be caused by mites and results in the contraction of minor ailments leading to a high level of sickness absence. The solution seems to be a high standard of cleaning.

The Workplace (Health, Safety and Welfare) Regulations 1992 place duties on controllers of premises in respect of everything under their control. In the case of the owner or a multi-tenanted building, that may include all common services and facilities, and covers the health and safety of visitors and contractors, as well as occupants.

Regulations covering exposure to asbestos fibres could be relevant for many of the buildings of the 1960s and early 1970s, when asbestos was used as thermal and fire insulation. Asbestos can cause diseases such as asbestosis and mesothelioma many years after exposure.

Property managers must keep abreast of the continual introduction and updating of health and safety legislation. Good health and safety management can save money, ensure high morale among occupants and is an essential aspect of good customer service.

Environmental audits

In order to ensure high standards in the areas described, it is good practice to consider audits of systems and procedures at appropriate intervals. These can cover four areas:

- *Compliance* A compliance audit is usually technical and carried out to check compliance with legislation, guidelines and policies. The report gives the opportunity for experts to recommend improvements, even if the building meets all the compliance requirements.
- *Management* This tests the operation of the company's environmental policy objectives as well as providing the chance to consider process improvements.
- *Product* A product audit is mainly carried out in manufacturing industry. It considers the impact on the environment of the supply of materials, production processes and distribution of a product.
- *Liability* A liability audit would normally be carried out before the acquisition of land or buildings and needs to be undertaken in painstaking detail to ensure that the buyer knows all the details of previous ownership, usage and contamination.

All new buildings need to take account of the environmental impact, from concept and design, through construction, occupation and finally to demolition. Property owners should therefore become familiar with the Building Research Establishment Environmental Assessment Method (BREEAM) which provides guidance on minimizing the adverse environmental effects of buildings, both globally and locally.

A BREEAM certificate compares the performance of a building against a set of criteria as measured by independent assessors appointed by the British Research Establishment. The BREEAM scheme is intended to encourage best practice in design, operation and maintenance, highlight good buildings, set higher standards than required by law, and raise the awareness of designers, owners, occupants and managers about the possible adverse impact of buildings.

COMMUNITY RESPONSIBILITY

Good practice in the area of environment, health, safety and security is not just about compliance. It is also about a management philosophy that accepts wider community responsibility, and embraces the challenge to seek out new and better ways, so as to ensure the sustainability of the world's people and natural resources.

Notes

1. Porter, M.E. (1985) *Competitive Advantage* (New York: Free Press).
2. Prokesch, S.E. (1995) 'Competing on Customer Service: An Interview with British Airway's Sir Colin Marshall', *Harvard Business Review*, November–December p. 104.
3. Ibid.
4. Tony Edwards (1996) Building and Estates Manager, The Home Office, *Property Week Supplement*, November.
5. Alessandra, T. (1990) *Relationship Strategies*, Set of six sound cassettes by Convention Cassettes Unlimited, Palm Desert, California (also available on video – 1993) (Chicago: Nightingale Connant).
6. Jeremy Boyes, Property Director, Gatwick Airport Limited, BAA plc. 1 November 1996, Internal launch day.
7. Andrew Rabeneck (1996) Director of European Facilities, Salomon Brothers, *Property Week Supplement*, November.
8. Confederation of British Industry (1996) *Partnership Sourcing in Action* (London: CBI).
9. Geoff Smith, UK Purchasing Manager, Nissan.

9 The Partnership Approach to Development Management

This book does not cover property development but, because construction, often through refurbishment, affects a tenant as well as the owner, the following question is relevant. How can an owner or owner's representative become more expert at procuring and managing the construction process and how can this add value to the tenant? Part of the answer lies in an owner's ability to work in partnership with the construction industry, to reduce costs and build facilities which better meet their needs.

Development is a complex, capital-intensive and risky activity which requires a high degree of management skill and experience. It usually involves a developer or owner-occupier bringing together a wide range of specialist consultants and contractors, often working in confined spaces around a tenant. Conversion and refurbishment tend to be particularly demanding and specialist activities.

The developer must deploy the pivotal skills needed to ensure the success of a project. The development manager is the person who identifies the commercial opportunity, defines the customer and the customer's needs, and then specifies the project to meet those needs. In short, the development manager identifies the opportunities to create value, and then evolves practical solutions to realise that value through the design and construction of appropriate facilities.

When considering the creation of value the question is: 'Value for whom?' More often than not, the primary value arises for the financial institution providing the capital and for the developer, as they are usually the main parties to the development. Value can be realised as a financial return for the fund, and cash proceeds of a sale for the developer.

For a tenant the value arises from the benefits the leased facility will bring to its business, and therein lies one of the main weaknesses of traditional development. Historically, much development work is speculative – the end-user is not known at the time of the development, and may only emerge after the building has been completed. This means that the development manager has to second-guess the likely needs of the tenant, and balance them against the needs of the funding instituation. It is not surprising that tenants often find that their facilities do not meet their needs.

Although many large companies own at least part of the property they occupy and from time to time become involved in development, only the largest, where property is part of their core business, have in-house development expertise. They include hotel and supermarket chains. For many of these companies the traditional speculative building does not provide the right fit with their business, and so they are forced to use in-house expertise to meet their needs.

However, most companies lack development management skills, and this can lead to unhappy results, usually because complexity is underestimated and proper project disciplines are not followed. In contrast, the professional development manager combines development expertise with the entrepreneurial and management skills needed to initiate, specify and deliver the project. Effective development managers have a real understanding of the construction industry and know how to work with the industry to achieve the required results at minimum cost and in the shortest possible time.

The construction of a building can be likened to the production of a car except a motor manufacturing plant is set up to produce thousands of cars whereas a property team is assembled for a one-off product. It is perhaps not surprising that production times and costs are more predictable for cars than for buildings.

THE UK CONSTRUCTION INDUSTRY

The construction industry in the UK is not renowned for high levels of performance and innovation. Many reasons are cited for this; a failure to adopt modern management and production techniques, a lack of training and skills development, a failure to embrace and exploit new technologies, a high proportion of casual labour, and conflict and contractual disputes at all levels.

Many industry observers believe that the lack of international competition in construction lies at the root of the problem. Research has shown that companies in other industries have reached world-class standards by facing up to intense competition that ignores national boundaries. This international rivalry drives rapid improvement in the quality and cost of products. Consider the advances in computers, hi-fi and cameras, or on a larger scale, in cars and aircraft. All of these products have shown dramatic improvement in sophistication, cost and quality over the past few decades, whereas the construction industry has made only modest improvements.

The absence of the fierce competition seen in world-class industries has left the construction industry with a legacy of problems which form barriers to change and improvement. Construction remains a fragmented industry of many small firms, largely operating on very low profit margins. Allied with a high rate of business failures, under-investment has prevented the industry from adopting the technologies, the skills and the modern management techniques that are needed to improve performance.

If the absence of competition is at the root of poor performance in UK construction, does the same situation exist in other countries? To examine this it is worth comparing the UK and US construction industries. In a recent study, BAA plc found a strong contrast in their efficiency and costs, resulting in a 30% lower out-turn construction cost in the US. The study clearly showed fundamental differences in the structures of the two industries. For example, in the US, far more design is carried out by contractors. The industry also uses a higher proportion of standard designs and components, has more efficient working practices which reduce the number of man-hours, and adopts more cost-effective space and design standards. The effect is a more efficient industry with lower costs than the UK's.

The BAA plc study supports the findings of Sir Michael Latham in his ground-breaking report on the UK construction industry, where he makes recommendations aimed at reducing building costs by 30% (*Constructing the Team*, 1995).[1] The essential goals to achieve this were a reduction in conflict, the adoption of a partnering approach and measures to increase efficiency.

Among the larger UK construction companies there is widespread recognition that the improvements are not just necessary but essential if the industry is to survive international competition in the home market. Some firms are making strenuous efforts to provide a more customer-focused service and are investing in the technologies and processes needed for efficient and cost-effective projects. They see improvements being achieved through closer relationships with clients, more effective project processes and a dramatic improvement in the skills base of the industry.

Construction companies also point out, quite rightly, that not all of the blame for their performance should be laid at their door. Their customers frequently contribute to the problem by being unclear about their requirements, unreasonable in their timescales and budgets and by making changes once the project is underway. These attitudes reflect poor development management and usually lead directly to increased costs, lower standards and late completion.

CONSTRUCTION AS A MANUFACTURING PROCESS

The design and construction of new buildings or the refurbishment of existing ones is undoubtedly a complex process involving the competing demands of tenants, designers, planners, contractors and suppliers. But other industries manage equally complex processes and deliver their products with greater certainty and customer satisfaction. Can the construction industry learn the key lessons about improvements and find practical ways of applying them?

Clearly buildings are not manufactured products and each building project has unique constraints determined by the location, the site conditions and the tenant's needs. But perhaps if the construction industry looks at its similarities with manufacturing rather than its differences it will begin to understand how manufacturing's approach can be used to deliver the buildings that tenants need at the right prices, on time and without defects.

The need for improved construction performance has been recognized particularly by clients such as hotels, supermarkets and airports whose buildings are an essential part of their business. Over the past decade many such clients have set about establishing their own development organizations to drive quality up and costs down.

Construction represents one element of development costs but has a knock-on effect on others such as fees and financing charges. The building owners that can cut construction costs without compromising quality are bound to enjoy a competitive advantage over those that adopt a 'business as usual' philosophy. The most sophisticated of this new breed of client are actively managing the whole development process, from market research, through design of components, production and after-care, to maintenance. They are thinking and acting like manufacturers in the pursuit of improved performance.

This approach to construction is applicable to any developer of buildings, large or small, but because the core of the problem is the need to change an industry it will naturally be easier for companies with large construction programmes.

IMPROVING PERFORMANCE

As the world's leading airport company spending more than £500 million per annum on construction of operational and commercial property, BAA plc realised that it had to find ways of improving the efficiency of its project processes if it was to continue to grow its business. Sir John Egan, Chief Executive, BAA plc, summarized the challenge:

> To make our £500 million go further each year we need to design and build to standards which match or better the best in the world. We want no delays, no changes, no cost overruns, no surprises, just a 100% predictable result every time we build. World-class performance is what BAA is now demanding of itself and its partners in the construction industry.[2]   (Issue 1, In Context, 1996)

"I SAID BRICK, NOT CURTAIN WALLING"

BAA plc began its drive for world-class performance by studying the best manufacturing companies and the methods that they are using to improve their products and their performance in the fiercely competitive environments in which they operate. Visits to companies successfully manufacturing a wide range of products, including cars, construction toys, aircraft and automotive parts, revealed some common themes:

- A clear understanding of customers' needs and the development of products that meet and even inform those needs.
- Use of standard components to achieve predictable assembly and performance and to reduce cost. Innovation is a deliberate and controlled process to minimize risk to performance and delivery.
- Defining and continuously improving processes to minimize waste.
- Investing in skilled people.
- Measuring performance because companies can only improve what they measure.
- Stable, integrated supply chains comprising the minimum number of first-rate suppliers with whom they have a partnering relationship. This approach is one of the keys to success.

In the following two years BAA plc developed these ideas with the construction industry into a simple strategy for continuously improving its projects towards its stated goal of world-class performance in capital investment.

Although the driving force behind the strategy is to reduce costs, it is recognized that this must be done by eliminating waste to avoid reducing the quality of projects. The strategy has four key elements.

Improving the product

The first part of the strategy is to improve the product that BAA plc provides for its customers – the airlines – and their passengers. If the company is to deliver appropriate airport facilities and commercial properties it has to understand the needs of the aviation industry in the 21st century. To that end the company has embarked on a programme of research to define air travel in the next century and the business services and technologies which will support it. And it is working with one of its major customers to research the factors which influence passengers' perceptions of quality in airport facilities and other buildings. BAA plc's objective is to become expert at providing adequate capacity and appropriate customer service with the minimum of new construction.

Improving services and components

The second part of the strategy is to work with suppliers to improve the quality of, and reduce the cost of, the services and components that BAA needs to design and construct its airports. An important ingredient in improving performances is to access the skills, the ideas and the energy of suppliers and put them to work at the heart of construction projects. This encourages relationships based on commitment, co-operation and common objectives. If construction clients go down the 'lowest bid from any supplier' route they should not be surprised if quality and out-turn price become prizes to fight over between the contractors, the designers and, of course, the client. That is why BAA plc is putting in place a supply chain that is dedicated to its construction programme. Simon Murray, the Managing Director of BAA plc Group Technical Services, has noted that:

> Ultimately it is hoped that the relationship between BAA and its partners will be so good that it will be difficult to distinguish our staff from those of our framework partners and all of us will be working to world best standards, and all of us will prosper; an appealing prospect I am sure you would agree.[3]
> (Presentation at BAA plc Projects Conference for Suppliers, 1996)

Through framework agreements BAA plc has contracted a small number of companies to supply the principal, high-value components for its facilities, such as lifts, escalators, chillers, carpets, seating, airbridges and concrete pavements. Standard components are esential in the move towards world-class construction efficiency as they cut out waste at the design and manufacturing stages. In the construction phase, delivery of predictable, easily assembled components can be closely controlled so the right items arrive just in time to be used, eliminating waste of materials, time and effort. BAA plc has reduced the number of design consultants and construction managers from more than 80 to just 30, and has introduced the Strive for Five programme to help encourage framework suppliers to make continuous improvement in their performance, year after year. The programme identifies five key improvement areas: cost, quality, time, safety and environment. Within each of these is a ladder of improvement targets that each supplier is encouraged to achieve. The lower rungs represent straightforward improvements, such as implementing quality management systems, whereas the upper rungs are more challenging. Suppliers are measured on their performance and progress to provide them with data and feedback. The ultimate target is that each supplier should reach world-best standards in each of the five improvement areas.

Improving the processes

The third part of BAA plc's strategy is to improve the processes by which projects are designed and constructed. The construction industry has a myriad of project processes which often reflect the narrow interests of one of the participants. BAA plc took all of these processes, gained an understanding of what best practice might look like and developed its own project process which is now in use across the business. As a project progresses from idea to reality it passes through a series of gateways where the scheme is challenged and assessed to see whether what is proposed is the right solution. There is heavy emphasis on front-end development management as this is where many of the cost savings are to be found. The introduction of the new process has been accelerated by training the consultants, contractors and BAA plc's own staff who are involved in projects.

The BAA plc project process is a step forward but it still reflects the traditional sequence of designing, procuring and constructing projects. The next challenge is to establish processes that ensure all of the skills and experience of suppliers are used in the earliest stages of design where they have the greatest impact. To understand how to achieve this BAA plc has embarked on a full-scale experiment in concurrent engineering.

The construction of a multi-storey car park at Heathrow was being used to test a manufacturing approach to design and construction, where designers, contractors and suppliers worked together as an integrated production unit. The result is that design work was done only once and the construction process was greatly simplified. This has significantly reduced the cost and duration of the project and also improved predictability.

Improving skills

The final part of the strategy is to work with suppliers to improve the quality of all the people that work on BAA plc's projects. The skills and commitment of people are essential for success and it is only by attracting, developing and retaining the best people that the company will succeed with its ambitious programme. As Graham Matthews, the Project Services Director of BAA plc Group Technical Services, commented:

> Everything we are doing to make the step change in construction relies on the people we and our supplier partners employ. They have to be the right people, they have to be thoroughly motivated and they have to be well trained. This applies equally to our own people; we know only too well that we, the client, can let the side down. We are engaged in a comprehensive training exercise for suppliers that explains what we are trying to achieve and how we are going to do it. And we have developed training packages for our own staff and ways to monitor and measure their effectiveness.[4]
>
> (Presentation at BAA plc Projects Conference for Suppliers, 1996)

BAA plc's training programme covers technical, business and personal skills and ranges in intensity from simple half-day workshops to a company-focused MBA. Most of the programme is based on open learning and is available to suppliers as well as BAA plc employees. The aim is to create teams of people with high standards of skills and this can only be achieved through common training and learning.

Although BAA plc is a large company with a major construction programme, the principles and processes that are employed can be applied to great effect on the most modest of projects. Efficient construction begins with a clear understanding of the product that is to be built and with confidence gained from solutions which are known to work. Efficiency is obtained by following simple and explicit processes and by minimizing tasks which add no value. Success in any venture also needs the motivation of the best people to tackle the task.

THE FUTURE OF THE CONSTRUCTION INDUSTRY

Few would disagree that the construction industry is going through a period of intense change that is challenging the structures, values and practices of the past. The industry has shrunk considerably from its peak in the late 1980s and is now operating at a level where it may be unable to meet any significant upturn in demand. If this turns out to be the case, the demand will suck in overseas competition as the UK industry is unable to meet supply requirements. This competition may produce a better product and be more efficient; if so it will secure a competitive stronghold that may unseat UK companies that do not drive to achieve what their clients require; lower costs without compromising quality.

There is also a strong movement among the larger, property-owning clients to drive change and improvement themselves, dictating how the industry should perform through integrated supply chains and sophisticated process control, rather than procuring their facilities as a consumer. It might only take a demonstrable improvement in cost and quality by one client to prove that it can be done. If a number of clients were to achieve this in concert the drive towards an improved construction industry might become unstoppable.

Whatever the future brings, one thing seems certain. If companies in the industry do not change and improve they will eventually be displaced by competitors that are better able to meet the increasing demands of their clients.

SUMMARY

This chapter has described one example of how a client can become more expert in procuring and managing construction projects. It is those building owners who are able to make this improvement step-change that will best be able to stand up to competitive pressures by providing tenants with buildings at lower capital and operating costs. In taking this route developers are starting to recognize the good sense in adopting what the *Tomorrow's Company* research has called an 'inclusive' approach in which a company 'works actively to build reciprocal relationships with customers, suppliers and other key stakeholders, through a partnership approach' (Mark Goyder, *News from the Centre*, 1997).[5]

Notes

1. Sir Michael Latham (1995) *Constructing the Team* (London: HMSO).
2. Sir John Egan, Chief Executive, BAA plc. Issue 1, In Context, September 1996 (BAA plc).
3. Simon Murray, Managing Director, BAA Group Technical Services. Presentation at BAA plc Projects Conference for Suppliers, '21st Century Airports', September 1996.
4. Graham Matthews, Project Services Director, BAA Group Technical Services. Presentation at BAA plc Projects Conference for Suppliers, '21st Century Airports', September 1996.
5. Mark Goyder, Director, Centre for Tomorrow's Company, *News from the Centre – The Journal of the Centre for Tomorrow's Company*, p. 1, January 1997.

10 Marketing

This chapter considers marketing as a management discipline and its position in a property-owning organization. Tenants and potential tenants also give their views on the approach to property marketing which is recommended in this chapter.

WHAT IS MARKETING?

Almost every text on marketing begins along the lines 'marketing is ...'. Despite marketing being so often discussed, it is rarely well understood and, in concept at least, can cover a broad range of issues.

The most commonly-held view, particularly in the property industry, is that marketing is merely about the creative functions of promotion and selling. Certainly these are important elements, but they only represent parts of marketing. Customers will not buy products or services which do not meet their needs – whatever creative promotional activities are employed. Marketing therefore has to be about delivering what the customer wants, rather than merely trying to sell what the organization happens to make.

Peter Drucker, probably the most influential writer on management, makes the point clearly:

> True marketing starts out with the customers, their demographics, relative needs and values. It does not ask 'What do we want to sell?', it asks 'What does the customer want to buy?'[1]   (Drucker, *Management*, 1979)

Marketing is the management function which has responsibility for understanding what customers want, which, in turn, should drive what the company produces. Marketing therefore has a critical strategic role in creating a sustainable business and long-term wealth for an organization.

Sir Colin Marshall, the first Chairman of The Marketing Council, established in 1995 by leading UK industrialists 'to help British businesses increase wealth creation and competitiveness through marketing' stated:

> Marketing means understanding and satisfying customers. It is the key to wealth creation. For so important an activity, it is poorly understood.[2]
> (Marshall, *Creating Wealth for Britain through Marketing*, 1995)

The Marketing Council defines marketing as:

> Any activity which creates customer satisfaction, or helps to anticipate and satisfy customer needs profitably.[3]
> (The Marketing Council, *Creating Wealth for Britain through Marketing*, 1995)

The Council proposes that by moving towards *pan-company marketing* companies can create a customer culture with a greater, more imaginative, focus on customer satisfaction which increases market share, creates new markets and *transforms companies by raising their standards*. This promotes the idea of marketing as an all encompassing management philosophy – *an attitude of mind which places the customer at the very centre of business* according to Barwell[4] ('The Marketing Concept', 1965) – which permeates all aspects and levels of the organization, thus covering any activity which creates customer satisfaction.

Marketing should be an integral part of any business although the specific roles of those employed in marketing will vary from industry to industry, depending on the nature of the products or services, and the maturity of the markets. It will also vary from company to company depending on the importance placed on the function within the organization.

PROPERTY MARKETING TRADITIONS

Within the property industry, it is rare to find marketing playing the central role that it does in most other industries, particularly those in consumer markets. For the developers and owners of commercial property, marketing is often seen merely as an activity to promote the company's image and to sell or let its buildings. It is rarely thought of as a distinct and important function with the capability to add value through understanding markets, helping to design products and identifying future areas of new business and growth.

This is due to a number of factors:

1. Commercial property has not historically been considered as a consumer product for a large customer base, but as a high-value investment product traded between relatively few buyers. Most developers of commercial property have seen their customers as being the purchasers of this investment product.
2. With commercial property viewed as an investment, the occupier has not been regarded as a customer but, rather, as a component of the product, albeit one without which the value of the product is significantly reduced. Indeed, in many pre-funded transactions, the completed product (that is, the building), can often be sold before it is known whether an occupier, who actually sustains its value, will be found.

3. The existence of commercial property brokers and advisors has meant that owners have traditionally used these external resources for their marketing.
4. A fourth, and perhaps less tangible factor, is the more traditional culture of the commercial property sector which tends to use entrepreneurial skills to maximize an opportunity without first using marketing in its fullest sense to understand the drivers for competitive advantage.

Therefore, the customer focused ethos which has dominated management thinking in corporations in consumer markets, and which has led to the emergence of marketing as a distinct management function, has not developed in commercial property owners.

Nevertheless, the extremely difficult market conditions faced by developers and owners in the early 1990s which resulted in a large oversupply of product in some sectors, and collapse of occupier demand, forced them to re-examine all areas of their businesses.

Property owners of all types, from individual house owners to institutions holding large commercial portfolios, were faced with what to many was a new experience; falling values coupled with significant voids in rental income, and high fixed overhead costs associated with maintaining vacant property. Resulting from this was a more dedicated, specialist, approach to certain marketing activities, in areas such as promotion, sales and letting, with a number of companies establishing dedicated in-house teams targeted at reducing void levels. This undoubtedly increased the recognition of the value of marketing expertise within these businesses.

Similarly, greater attention was paid to more sophisticated market research following some of the very painful lessons learned in the early 1990s through the lack of a sufficiently structured, analytical approach to understanding the demands of the occupiers of buildings.

Whilst many of these changes have been sustained, the property industry still has some catching up to do, compared with other industries, before the full benefits of marketing can be enjoyed. Those property owners that are prepared to take on board all aspects of marketing, not only those to do with selling the product, will find their financial reward through higher levels of occupancy and greater occupier satisfaction leading to growth in values.

THE APPROACH TO PROPERTY MARKETING

The approach that BAA plc adopted for marketing property is one which would be equally relevant to other property owners, and indeed to other industries. It encompasses a number of issues.

Identifying the customer

Marketing should really begin with the strategic question 'What areas of business should we be in and why?' The answer will differ from company to company but for BAA plc it was straightforward; described by Peter Clegg, the Head of Property Marketing, as:

> Using core skills to develop new facilities at our airports which support and add value to our customers' businesses whilst increasing shareholder value.[5] (Peter Clegg, Head of Property Marketing, BAA plc, 1996)

A property owner must clearly understand both macro-economic issues, such as the political, cultural, social, legal and trading constraints which influence a business to locate in a particular country or region, as well as micro-economic factors such as local incentives, labour supply, housing and transport. These types of considerations are crucial to any location decision, which is inevitably expensive for the business concerned, disruptive to employees, and affects the image portrayed to partners and customers. It is also a decision which cannot be reversed easily in the short term.

In respect of BAA plc property, the target audience was split into two categories:

- current tenants whose businesses needed to be retained if the company was to continue to prosper; and
- potential customers whose needs must be understood if the company was to win their business and grow new sources of income.

Following this initial categorization, the next steps involved, first, understanding which businesses were 'air related' under the local authority planning constraints, and, secondly, from this very large but clearly defined group of companies, establishing a priority target audience whose businesses would benefit from being closer to their core operations at the airports as well as sustaining the airport's growth and efficiency. This was undertaken for each distinct area of business encompassing not only cargo and aircraft maintenance facilities but also passenger, airline and statutory authority support facilities.

The resultant database provided accurate profiles on several hundred companies which satisfied the air-related criteria, some of which were already located on the airports, some in the surrounding areas, and some based in cities or their suburbs. Changing technology, for example, might make the need for an airline to have its sales force based in a prime central city location far less relevant than was originally the case.

Provided that the information put onto the database is collated in an ordered manner, it is then possible to prioritize and search under a wide variety of criteria, such as size, number of employees, urgency of potential property requirement, geographical location, and so on.

Understanding customers and their property needs

Having defined the customer base the next, and far more important, step was to understand their businesses, the importance of property as a function within them, and the costs they could afford to allocate to it. In respect of airports, the type of facilities can range from hangars and transit sheds, commercial offices, industrial units, catering facilities, and so on. Unless the potential customer's requirements are clearly prioritized, the result is likely to be the all-too-common speculative development of buildings that try to be all things to all people.

BAA plc took three basic steps to identify customer needs; research, development of a customer contact programme and installing the right information management system.

Background research

Research can start at the most basic level – with contact names and addresses of companies – but needs to be developed into a far more detailed profile of each target company to provide an understanding of its corporate structure, principal business activity, financial performance, strategy for growth, culture, key personnel and, of course, existing property interests.

Each company will have different characteristics that must be understood. Some might be driven by cost constraint which overrides any need to be close to their customers, and hence they will migrate to cheaper locations. Others, perhaps in a service business, might wish to be alongside their clients in prime locations.

Knowing the corporate structure of a particular organization allows an understanding to be developed of the relationship between the parent company, its subsidiaries, and its business partners. Given the diverse and complex evolution of many organizations, this information may enable an existing relationship with one part of the business to be developed in order to do business with another.

A clear understanding of the issues affecting the markets in which a business operates can provide an essential insight into potential changes which may affect its property strategy. As Denis Taylor, the General Manager for Property at British Airways plc, noted in relation to the Compass Centre at Heathrow:

> By taking time to understand the processes and pressures involved in our business, BAA has been able to provide a highly-flexible complex of buildings close

to our sphere of operations on the airport, which allow us to maximise the cost efficiency of the various business units which operate within it.[6]
(Denis Taylor, General Manager Property, British Airways plc, 1996)

For effective communication, it is essential to establish who the principal decision-makers are within a target company, and, in many cases, this may not be the person responsible for property issues on a day-to-day basis. In some companies, the property personnel are not represented on the board, and may report through other functions, such as finance or personnel. In other cases, the managing director may deal with property issues personally.

When assessing a company's property needs, it is also important to consider factors such as where senior executives and their staff live, and any other business interests which they may have as this could be an influence on their choice of location. The thought of a 15-minute drive to work, or good public transport connections, may be a deciding factor in any company's relocation decision. Filippo Rotunno, the Admin/Personnel Manager for the UK and Ireland at Alitalia, commented:

In seeking to add value to our business by encouraging us to move our operation to Heathrow, BAA worked hard to address a number of transportation and life style preconceptions which existed amongst our staff *vis-à-vis* accessing and operating from a very different business environment on the airport to that we have traditionally enjoyed in the suburbs of London.[7]
(Filippo Rotunno, Admin/Personnel Manager UK and Ireland, Alitalia, 1996)

The research pieces together a comprehensive profile on each target company, including information about all its existing property assets, such as the building type, size, location, tenure, density of occupation, and lease expiry dates, as well as its future business plans. Based on the firm foundation this knowledge gives, it is then possible to initiate a programme of property development which will meet the needs of a particular business over a period of time. This should enable the active property owner to increase its market share relative to its existing customers, and to exploit fully new business from potential customers within its defined target audience.

When assessing the time and cost spent in properly researching potential customers' requirements, it is important to remember that the planning and construction of any new building takes not only a relatively long time compared with the development of other products, but also has a very long life and cannot easily be replaced or altered if occupiers' requirements change.

Research costs, when compared with the overheads and lost revenue which can be incurred when a completed building remains unlet for any significant period, are very good value. For example, a 5000 m^2 building let at £200 per m^2 costs over £80 000 in lost revenue for every month it remains vacant in terms of rent alone, to which must be added the liability for empty rates, security, and maintenance of the mechanical and electrical services, not to mention promotion costs and management time.

Developing a customer contact programme

Although thorough and accurate research is important, it can only provide the foundation for a programme of direct contact in order to understand the evolving requirements of customers. There are various ways in which customers' changing attitudes, needs and preferences can be identified and understood, ranging from personal meetings to customer surveys and events.

Having prioritized the target audience, there is no substitute for personal contact, and a structured programme of meetings has to be one of the single most important elements of any property marketing strategy. These meetings must focus, not on selling, but on seeking ways to add value to a tenant's business. This will help engender a true spirit of partnership that in the long run will be to the benefit of both businesses.

Clearly, there is a limit to the number of potential customers that can be approached through personal contact but, provided the original targeting is properly researched, it should be possible, unlike in many mass markets, to build good personal relationships which can provide the foundation for successful long-term and mutually profitable business partnerships. Bob Taylor, the European Director of American Airlines, stated:

> We have appreciated BAA's approach of visiting us regularly to find out what we are up to and to keep us informed about future property projects. Through this programme, we can work together to ensure that my company's evolving needs are well understood.[8]　(Bob Taylor, European Director, American Airlines, 1996)

All too often property managers, perhaps because they work in a specialized profession, can make the mistake of believing they have a better idea of what the customer wants than the customer and, whether consciously or not, stop listening to customers' views. At this point, the flexibility and suitability of the final product will inevitably begin to decline.

The use of customer surveys as a marketing information tool is not as well-focused as personal interviews, but can produce good background knowledge of customer requirements provided that the objectives are clear, and their limitations are recognized. In respect of any company's existing tenants, this provides a good source of information which is not readily accessible by competitors. It has the added benefit of rightly making the customer feel a recognized and valued contributor to the landlord's property business.

In order to help maintain good two-way communication about property issues, BAA plc has established a programme of events, from formal business briefings, seminars and conferences to informal gatherings, which provide valuable opportunities to meet customers outside their immediate working environment. When dealing with a clearly defined market such as that at or

"UNDERSTANDING CUSTOMERS' NEEDS"

close to an airport, this has the added benefit of allowing a number of customers to talk to each other socially, stimulating ideas and relationships which would otherwise be prevented by day-to-day pressures of work.

Information management

If customer focused marketing is to be an integral part of a long-term business strategy, it is essential that appropriate information management systems be established to allow customer data to be used effectively. All too often, the value of extremely useful and costly work is not maximized, or the material lost altogether, because of poor information systems. Clearly, such systems must be able to store data in a practical form, as well as allowing it to be used as a proactive business tool.

BAA plc developed a personalized information system, modelled on Lotus Notes, to provide an integrated customer database and workflow tool which is networked across all its airports. All the customer data gathered by the property teams at the airports is recorded in an easily understandable format, and made available throughout the company.

For example, a property manager in Glasgow, meeting one of his cargo customers such as DHL, TNT or Federal Express, all of which might have property interests at other airports, has instant access to details of any other

meetings which might have taken place with another part of that organization at, say, Gatwick or Heathrow airport, only a few hours earlier. This not
only avoids possible duplication of work through poor communication, but
also creates an immediate impression of efficiency and professionalism with
the customer. Bob Drabb, Managing Director for Europe of LSG Skychef,
commented:

> It is refreshing to deal with an organization in BAA that has effective internal
> communications amongst its managers, who come to meetings with clear agen-
> das which are focused on helping us to solve our business needs and do not
> waste our time in covering the same ground again.[9]
>
> (Bob Drabb, Managing Director Europe of LSG Skychef 1996)

Matching product with demand

A comprehensive understanding of customer needs is of course only valuable if the company then develops a strategy which enables it to prosper
through delivering products which match that need, in the right location, at
the right time and on the right financial terms.

The marketing team must therefore liaise closely with other development
management and financial functions within the organization to create an
effective product line for the end-user. The research database is then used to
ensure that the right decisions are taken all along the line as far as customers are concerned. As part of BAA plc's development programme established under the Property Challenge initiative, each new development or
refurbishment scheme is rigorously analyzed to ensure that it meets the
company's objective to 'support and add value to its customers' businesses'.

Achieving this objective is not only about the quality and flexibility of a
building, but also about the support services provided and the terms upon
which the space is made available. This might involve the provision of a regular shuttle bus between the property and the central terminal areas where
the airlines have their core operational functions. Similarly, customers are
offered the length of lease to suit their business plan; after all, why tie an
occupier into a 15- or 20-year lease if their business planning process can
only accurately forecast revenue and expenditure over the next five?

Research showed some occupiers expressing frustration at having to
lease large areas of a building to provide conference and meeting room
facilities when these were only occupied for a small part of each day. As a
result, certain developments were designed to incorporate such facilities as
a common resource that tenants could book, for when they were actually
required, and pay for them by the hour. This substantially reduced the area
they had to lease and significantly reduced their annual fixed costs. For
BAA plc, the reward is the prospect of higher levels of tenant retention.

Obviously, every occupier will have different requirements and it is
never possible to meet all of these in any one project. However, by

demonstrating an awareness of the practical difficulties encountered by occupiers in the daily running of their businesses, and by finding solutions to at least some of them, the landlord is perceived to be acting in a spirit of partnership. This is exemplified by the comment of Robin Bevan, the Country Manager for UK and Ireland at Cathay Pacific Airways:

> BAA encouraged and assisted us to look at our potential move as an integrated business decision, encompassing more efficient working practices through improved space planning, advanced information management systems, and comprehensive facilities management. Travel costs, staff facilities and other issues important to our staff were analyzed. In this way, we could show substantial savings in our fixed overheads to our parent organisation, thus creating a proper business rationale for the move, rather than simply comparing existing rent and rates against proposed rent and rates.[10]
> (Robin Bevan, Country Manager UK and Ireland, Cathay Pacific Airways Ltd, 1996)

An effective property marketing function should be able to provide prospective tenants with a cost–benefit analysis of a proposed move, both as far as the company is concerned and for its staff. In many cases, relocation of staff, or the potential loss of existing staff, will be the ultimate deciding factor in whether a move takes place. The softer issues also need to be analyzed; are there sufficient local shops and restaurants; is the environment clean and uncongested; and are there sufficient houses, schools and recreational facilities nearby?

Product promotion

Having invested considerable time, resources and capital in building or refurbishing a property, it is vital to ensure that an integrated communication and promotional campaign is in place throughout the project.

The awareness that both prospective occupiers and the business community as a whole have of any property owner is largely influenced by the perception gained from publicized new initiatives, whether they relate to the existing portfolio, new management initiatives or new developments. The production of promotional material, advertising, and other means of increasing awareness that are acknowledged to be professional and of a high quality will ensure that the message is as good as the product.

Any successful property owner should establish a clear identity for its buildings which sets it apart from its competitors, and which reflects a clear, highly-focused, business strategy. The essence of the owner's values should be mirrored through the promotional campaign. Traditionally, many property owners have taken a back seat as far as promotion is concerned and have allowed others to shape the way in which its products have been marketed. As a result, promotion has been inclined to reflect a deal-driven culture with the occupier 'offered the opportunity' to accept a building, and the supplier 'prepared to offer it' at a pre-specified price.

Typically, there are four basic stages in establishing a process for a promotional campaign: planning, preparation, implementation and review.

PROMOTIONAL CAMPAIGNS

Planning

The approach to marketing outlined in this chapter emphasizes the need to regard marketing as an integral part of the production of any property product from start to finish, and this is equally true when considering a promotional campaign. Brochures and advertising campaigns which are planned retrospectively once the product has been completed are fundamentally missing the point.

From the early definition of the customer base and an understanding of their needs, the promotional material used such as information packs, brochures, advertisements, the Internet and presentations, can be geared to convey the messages which are important to the future occupier. The strategy for any promotion has to be based on a thorough understanding of the product, its position in the market, the benefit it offers to potential consumers, and its position against competitors.

Awareness of any new product needs to be raised progressively as that product evolves from inception through to completion. All those involved in the success of the project – not only the design team – should understand how it is being positioned in the marketplace and the critical success factors. A strong brand for the project, with which people can identify, is important.

In order to be effective and to retain consistency, each stage of the promotional campaign needs to be programmed so that it dovetails with each stage of the project itself.

Preparation

Promotional material of whatever description often represents the first projection of a new scheme to the external markets and customers. Careful and comprehensive briefing for those involved in designing the material is therefore needed to ensure that the overall objectives are understood. It is easy at this stage for the property owner's team to have become so immersed in the project that they wrongly assume new consultants can easily catch up with the learning process which may have evolved over many months. If the material produced fails to position the product correctly, a large proportion of the potential customer base may not be reached.

It is also important that design consultants become part of the team and feel a real sense of ownership, as in the following comments by the managing director of Roger Felton Associates:

> In helping BAA Property to establish a brand for its products distinct from the many other core functions which exist within the BAA Group, we worked alongside the property teams, to not only understand their business objectives and culture, but to help them to understand our business and the processes involved. In this way, we managed to continually refine our service and the quality of material we produced to make it more effective both as regards cost and impact.[11]
> (Roger Felton, Design Consultants Roger Felton Associates, 1996)

Implementation

The implementation and rolling out of a promotional campaign should not be regarded as simply a case of undertaking mailshots to all and sundry within the target audience, or carrying out a major advertising campaign. Continued regard should be had for the current priorities of the customer to ensure that the relationships built up during the research stages are not jeopardized. For example, a particular business which has expressed strong interest in the product may simply not be able to give it due consideration during certain periods of the year such as when business plans are being drawn up for the next financial period, as this will dominate that business above all else.

Equally, the relationship between, say, an advertisement or PR campaign and direct contact must be considered. Is it better to raise awareness by running the advertisement, followed by a meeting with the customer, or to see the customer first, then, once the campaign is underway, make them aware that others are also being targeted?

All members of the marketing team should understand their role in the process and how that role affects the actions of others in the team. The responses received have to be carefully co-ordinated to avoid misunderstandings occurring or, worse still, the fragmentation of the campaign, with individuals pursuing particular leads which do not fulfil the original objectives.

The decision-making process

To enable maximum success to be achieved, the marketing strategy must incorporate a clear understanding of how initial interest can be converted into signed agreements with the end-users. For example, which person or group from within the customer's organization will have final responsibility for approving the transaction, and what procedures will that company need to go through in order to present a satisfactory business case to gain this approval? Many multinational companies have extremely complex processes which have to be adhered to before any decisions can be taken, and whilst a particular project may be high on the owner's list of priorities, it may not assume the same importance to the potential customer. The marketing team must be in a position to help the prospective customer through this period by responding to requests for data and information in different forms, and by providing coherent and objective advice where necessary.

Clearly, in order to achieve this, the team also has to make sure that processes are in place to gain approvals in their own organization so that clear directives can be given.

Review

The experiences gained from any promotional campaign can only be used to increase competitive advantage in the future if a thorough audit is undertaken retrospectively to ensure that the process is improved constantly. All too often, each marketing exercise is treated as a totally new project without reference to the lessons of the past.

The results of this audit, which should examine every stage of the marketing process, must then be communicated to all members of the team involved in the project, including the consultants.

ACHIEVING SUCCESS

The whole objective of pursuing this type of structured approach to marketing is to convert existing or latent demand into mutually-profitable transactions for both the owner and the occupier, by producing the right product. The success of any marketing approach will be judged primarily on the profit which is actually produced by the project when compared to the original business plan projections.

The central issue to bear in mind is that best practice property marketing is about understanding and satisfying customers and, through that relationship, building long-term profitable and sustainable business partnerships.

Notes

1. Peter Drucker (1979) *Management* (London: Pan).
2. Sir Colin Marshall (1995) 'Creating Wealth for Britain through Marketing' (The Marketing Council, Maidenhead).
3. The Marketing Council (1995) 'Creating Wealth for Britain through Marketing'.
4. C. Barwell (1965) 'The Marketing Concept', in Wilson, A. (ed.) *The Marketing of Industrial Products* (London: Hutchinson).
5. Peter Clegg, Head of Property Marketing, BAA plc, internal communication 1996.
6. Denis Taylor, General Manager Property, British Airways plc, personal correspondence 1996.

7. Filippo Rotunno, Admin/Personnel Manager, UK and Ireland, Alitalia, personal correspondence 1996.
8. Bob Taylor, European Director, American Airlines, personal correspondence 1996.
9. Bob Drabb, Managing Director Europe, LSG Skychef, personal correspondence 1996.
10. Robin Bevan, Country Manager UK and Ireland, Cathay Pacific Airways Limited, personal correspondence 1996.
11. Roger Felton, Managing Director, Design Consultants Roger Felton Associates, internal correspondence 1996.

11 Airport Retailing: A Case Study

This chapter considers one of the world's leading customer-driven property management businesses – retailing at BAA plc's London, Scottish and US airports – in the context of the Building Blocks described in previous chapters.

It looks in particular at the impact of changes that took place between 1988 and 1997 after BAA plc was formed by the 1987 privatisation of the British Airports Authority, and highlights how the approach may be applicable to more conventional property businesses. In this context retailing encompasses shops, catering, retail services and car parking.

Airport retailing, particularly at Heathrow and Gatwick, has been one of the success stories of the 1990s. Commentators tend to contrast airports with the high street by focusing on the novelty of location and the absence of traditional rental agreements in favour of concession agreements where the landlord's income is related in whole or in part to the retailer's turnover. In fact, concession agreements were in place well before airport retailing became successful, and the travel-based nature of the location has a long history. Many other factors have driven the success of the strategy.

Travel retailing is nothing new; the location of many towns and cities was influenced by travel needs such as river crossings, harbours, stopping places for horse-drawn coaches and railway junctions. All required support functions, from overnight accommodation for coach passengers to chandlers for provisioning ships. Shops were a natural part of the commercial activities that grew up at these places. The itinerant peddlers that still climb aboard trains and buses in the developing world are in many ways the forerunners of airport retailing! They are meeting a demand by displaying their wares before the travelling public.

BLOCK 1   DEFINING THE CUSTOMER

Concession agreements have long been a feature of airport retailing, and because of the shared nature of the arrangement it would be easy to assume that this was a successful formula. BAA plc's experience, prior to

1988, showed that such agreements did not in themselves create a sustainable customer focused business.

The central problem was that the shops at the airports were not dedicated to meeting the needs of their customers, the passengers. Specialist retail outlets were developed by BAA plc's concessionaires without first considering how shoppers might respond to them. Indeed these bland and uninteresting businesses also occupied a major proportion of the airport retail space. Furthermore, because retailers were unique, it was not possible to benchmark customer service and pricing performance against the high street. This allowed the airport retailer to charge higher prices which in turn gave the landlord, BAA plc, a higher margin on sales.

BAA plc also had rigid tendering procedures which awarded sites to the highest bidders: effectively the same approach commonly used in the high street. This, and the acceptance of non-benchmarked airport specialists, ensured that high-street retailers in general, and certain types in particular, were likely to lose tenders to the higher-margin airport specialists.

The policy meant less choice for consumers and hence a lower spend, and the airport owner's willingness to accept the highest bid led to a very small number of companies dominating British airport retailing. In 1980, the then British Airports Authority had only eight concessionaires, but by 1997 this had increased to 200. This may have parallels in the increasing dominance of shopping centres by a relatively small core of major multiples that can provide landlords with the financial covenant that they require.

A continual cycle of re-tendering led to concession percentages rising steadily. This gave rise to some growth in landlord income, but at the expense of customer service since the retailers were forced to concentrate on maximizing their margin through reducing staff numbers and increasing prices rather than by maximizing sales through satisfying the customer. Public opinion of airport retailing was consequently very low and this was reflected in adverse press reports.

Not only was the airport passenger dissatisfied, BAA plc's other customer, the retailer partner, was too. The struggle to win contracts not only led to retailers providing poor service, but also to making bids that maintained turnover but offered them little or no profit. This generated confrontation between landlord and concessionaire and made co-operation and teamwork very difficult, if not impossible.

BLOCK 2   RESEARCHING WHAT THE CUSTOMER WANTS

In 1987 the BAA plc retail business looked healthy on the surface, with steadily increasing income generated by growing margins and flattered by growth in passenger numbers. The problem was the landlord's lack of real understanding of the underlying issues seen from both the retailers' and shoppers' points of view. This need for retail knowledge is important at airports and probably even more so at traditional shopping centres.

The financial success of airport retailing masked serious problems; the contractual novelty of large concession agreements was not structured to create a customer focused business and thereby maximize performance. Changes needed to be made.

Drivers for change

The factors that encouraged BAA plc to change its approach to retailing will not all necessarily be applicable to other businesses, but many will be. BAA plc was lucky enough to have had a multiplicity of drivers for change. This encouraged a total review of the retail business and a subsequent managerial restlessness that ensures that change and improvement are now continuous. The threat to town centre retailing from out-of-town centres may well justify a similar radical review of the way shopping property is managed.

Establishing retail as a core activity

Airports throughout the world should be capable of generating a significant proportion of their revenue from retailing. In many cases, however, this income is viewed as peripheral to the core business and not given sufficient priority or management attention. Establishing retail as a core business and not purely as a flow of income was central to turning it into a customer focused business.

One consequence of privatization was the regulation by the Civil Aviation Authority of BAA plc's other core income stream – airport charges – which were destined to rise at less than the rate of inflation. This reinforced the significance of retail as a core business and generated more pressure to review the way it was approached.

Shareholder profit growth expectations were a further pressure which meant that a strategy was needed for providing continuous growth in retail income. As the historical approach to increasing this income had given rise to so many problems, a different and potentially more difficult route needed to be followed. As Sir John Egan observed on joining BAA plc as Chief Executive in 1990 and reviewing the retail business: 'Sustainable growth in this business will only come through satisfying the customer.'

At this point, it was to BAA plc's advantage that there were concession agreements in place because these provided the base from which to grow performance-driven income in partnership with retailers (see Annex 1). This may be more difficult for companies whose income is derived from traditional leases with fixed rents and periodic, market-driven reviews.

Research

Research showed that BAA plc's retail business partners were dissatisfied, and the same story was told by passengers through public opinion surveys. It is doubtful whether many property owners have the measurements or benchmarks in place to detect such problems, but for BAA plc it was clear that further growth would only come from a new partnership approach, to maximize sales through satisfying customers.

Extensive market research took place across all airport terminals to establish an appropriate letting strategy for each area. This resulted in a full understanding of the profile of different passengers and led to the creation of a new strategy, carefully targeted at each market sector. This involved quantitative research but also qualitative research through group discussions to establish attitudes and aspirations.

BLOCK 3   CREATING A MISSION FOR THE ORGANIZATION

The original retail strategy was established in 1989 and adopted immediately and, although it has been reviewed and updated regularly ever since, its fundamental thrust remains unchanged:

> The strategy gave clarity not only to what the business needed to achieve, but also to who would achieve it and how. Although in many ways deceptively simple, the strategy required a fundamental change in the way business was conducted and in the criteria on which decisions were made.[1]
>
> (Barry Gibson, Group Retail Director, BAA plc, 1996)

The strategy can be summarized as the five Ps:

Philosophy

The underlying philosophy was to meet the needs of airport customers, best summarized by the retail division's mission statement:

> We will create a world class retailing experience for all our customers

and the retail vision:

> Along with their main purposes of using an airport terminal, passengers have the right to expect good service and an extensive range of high quality and appropriate retailing activities as part of their airport experience. BAA intends to meet that expectation by providing a retail environment whereby each terminal operates as a market in which retail income can be increasingly generated by nationally and internationally recognized retailers, caterers and other agencies who will compete for and improve the available business using service, quality, price and promotional techniques to attract customers.

People

The retail management team needed to be restructured to focus on the new challenges and opportunities. Subsequent reviews of the strategy addressed in greater detail issues of skills, competencies, training and development.

In addition, the strategy set goals for improving relationships with business partners through improved communication and consultation and a change in management style. An understanding of business partners' operations therefore became a more important qualification for staff than traditional property management skills.

Perception

The public's perception of airport retailing, reinforced by press comments, was of poor service and high prices. Such entrenched perceptions are difficult to shift, so strategies were needed that not only solved the problems but could be simply and forcefully communicated. The strategies were straightforward; price guarantees relating all prices and savings to high street prices with value for money and customer service measured through regular surveys.

Product

Research had shown that a radical shift would be needed in the range of retailers operating at the airports and in how these new partnerships were structured. The main aims were to boost competition by providing all types of consumers with a choice of outlets for particular products or services and to provide the reassurance of internationally or nationally known brand names.

To achieve this, BAA plc needed to shift away from tendered, margin-led allocation of space to a research-based considered approach where it established appropriate uses on the basis of customer need.

Premises

Historically, retail space had been developed in a piecemeal, opportunistic way. The interior design of the shopping areas needed to be greatly improved. The new strategy also required not only a dramatic increase in retail space but that each airport, and indeed terminal building, developed a letting strategy appropriate to its customer profile.

This approach is far more akin to the way in which a retailer will merchandise a store than to the way in which a landlord will traditionally let a high-street development.

IMPLICATIONS OF THE STRATEGY

Some important implications flow from the new strategy. A key point is the balance between sales volumes and concession margins. Income growth from concession contracts can come from either, and had historically come more from margin growth through regular tendering to generic airport retailers whose focus was growing their own margins rather than growing sales through satisfying the customer.

It was always understood that the new strategy with branded operators selling at high-street prices would lead to a reduction in average margins; the retailers' ability to meet customer needs, however, has led to a more than counterbalancing increase in sales volumes.

BLOCK 4   LEADERSHIP, EMPOWERMENT, TRAINING AND COMMUNICATION

The success of the strategy was reliant on clarity of purpose, effective leadership, well-motivated staff and excellent communication with growing numbers of retailers and passengers.

Measurable targets were established and became an important motivational tool for the members of the management team who were encouraged to take responsibility for achieving the strategic objectives. On the basis of a trial retail expansion in Terminal 4 at Heathrow, there was an overall target of increasing retail space at all BAA plc airports from 41 900 m^2 to 82 100 m^2 per annum. Sales and income targets were established by the return on investment required from each expansion scheme.

The move from rigid tendering procedures towards negotiated contracts with carefully selected operators required BAA plc to have a much enhanced set of skills. Accepting the highest bid requires no management skill but making a judgement about the long-term profitability of a business partner needs a manager who understands that retailer's business. The emphasis shifted from bureaucracy and control to selling, persuading and partnering.

Another implication of the partnership approach is the sharing of information both within and outside the organization. Once the retail strategy had the support of the BAA plc Board of Directors, it was communicated to all BAA plc retail staff at a two-day conference where the objectives, values and methods were clearly spelt out. The conference has since become an annual event and, as well as providing an opportunity to communicate important business initiatives, it has helped create a strong team culture which is critical if a large and geographically diffuse organization is to present a united front to the outside world.

The strategy was also communicated to business partners, again at a conference. This was important because many retailers, bearing in mind their experiences of the past, were sceptical that things had changed and new retailers also needed to be persuaded that airports were profitable places to open shops. The object of the conference was to communicate the strategy, establish understanding and create a foundation for profitable business partnerships based on trust. The initial conference for business partners revealed a degree of suspicion and dissatisfaction but as a result of the new partnership approach that has not been repeated at subsequent conferences.

BLOCK 5   PROCESS IMPROVEMENT AND INFORMATION MANAGEMENT

The retail strategy, focused on satisfying customers, has been a great success and the objective now is to improve processes, costs and management information so as to generate further profit by improving space productivity.

Service-based competition is likely to become an increasing feature of the property market in general, and the ability to continuously improve performance will be a necessity for any progressive landlord. Before improvements to processes can be made data is required on which to base judgements. This not only helps to highlight areas where improvement is required, but also enables the effect of new initiatives to be measured.

For example, the introduction of a worldwide money-back retail guarantee by BAA plc was generated by research that showed overseas passengers had concerns about buying items at UK airports because they did not know how they would return them if they were faulty. Improved shopper confidence has led to increased sales.

If rental income is performance-driven, then the landlord requires effective IT systems to provide regular sales performance data for each concessionaire so as to forecast, monitor and if necessary intervene. Furthermore, the concessionaire must be given regular information on footfall, performance benchmarks and levels of customer service performance.

It has already been highlighted that BAA plc's retail business, compared with most property management organizations, is data-rich. This data has been augmented by further market research and by the introduction of benchmarking to compare its financial and service performance with that of similar organizations. In the case of BAA plc, this is currently other airports around the world and the UK high street.

Information to improve performance naturally extends to financial measures, with cash flow and profit being important and the financial strength of the tenant being secondary. This is quite different from the traditional landlord's approach where often more emphasis is placed on the tenant's financial strength than on the income the business is likely to generate. In the longer term it is a sustainable tenant business that will add most to asset value.

Improved retail performance was also assisted by marketing, improved customer service and product development.

Marketing

The marketing of airport retailing has expanded from simple messages about savings and special offers to a nationwide TV advertising campaign, a loyalty-card programme now used by 100 000 regular passengers and the money-back customer guarantee. This guarantee means that a passenger can buy with confidence and return unwanted goods form anywhere in the world, free of charge and with a full 'no quibbles' refund.

This support is given without any charge to the retailer, but the nature of the concession agreement ensures that the benefits flow immediately to the landlord as well as to the retailer. Traditionally, loyalty cards and goods return policies have been operated by retailers but a landlord is often best placed to be the catalyst for the establishment of such schemes.

Customer service

Front-line shopping service at airports is generally provided by the concessionaire but this is no reason for the landlord not to be concerned about the levels of customer satisfaction. After all it is the owner's return on capital that is at stake. Therefore, work takes place with all retailers to help improve their service levels by running joint training programmes. This owner-led approach is likely to become the norm in major off-airport shopping centres as competition intensifies.

Furthermore, all terminals have shopping information desks funded by BAA and it has been made easy for shoppers to buy by providing a free-phone help-line which can also be used to pre-order goods. The next step in the drive to customer satisfaction is the setting up of a personal shopping service.

Again, the nature of concession agreements means that the expense of such initiatives can be justified by the increased sales and income that they generate.

Product development

A close understanding by a property owner of the market in which it and its partners operates enables a business to understand and pursue new opportunities.

BAA plc has used its specialist airport retailing knowledge to work with concessionaires on developing new product ranges as well as developing new retail concepts appropriate for airports. Examples include confectionery, souvenir and whisky specialist outlets.

Product strategies

It is possible to analyze the performance of any business in a variety of ways but, historically, the airport retail business looked at performance by outlet and location with no focus on product lines.

With the wealth of data available now, it is also possible to look at performance across outlets by product category; clothing, books, liquor, and so on. This enables strategies to be developed that not only maximize each outlet's performance, but also ensures that total sales for each product category are maximized at each airport. This reinforces the need to have managers who understand retail businesses.

Management structure

As a business develops, it is necessary to vary the emphasis given to different aspects of the business. In BAA plc this has meant a gradual move from developing and filling retail space to managing and maximizing the efficiency of that space. This cannot be achieved with a static management structure and changes are made so that the management team is always organized in a way that best suits the changing needs of the business. Management structures and skills always need to reflect the current challenges and opportunities, and this reinforces the need for a learning culture to be established where reacting to change becomes an everyday event.

BLOCK 6   MEASURING SUCCESS AND BENCHMARKING

Prior to 1989, the only performance information provided by retailers was a monthly sales and income statement received in the middle of the following month. The only information provided to retailers, if asked for, was monthly passenger forecasts.

BAA plc now receives weekly sales figures from every outlet by the Monday of the following week, sometimes broken down by key product area, and comparisons can now be made with the same retailers' high-street performance. In return, retailers can receive daily or weekly passenger forecasts, feedback on their customer service performance standards and benchmarked performance indicators from other outlets to enable them to compare their performance with the norm.

Retailer are now provided with information so they can tailor their merchandise range to specific flights; for example Bally will restock its shoe shops with appropriate styles and sizes for very short periods to cater for African or Japanese flights.

The average high-street landlord, by contrast, receives little information about its tenants' successes or failures, nor indeed gathers much information to provide in return. When a major retailer starts encountering problems it therefore tends to come as a surprise to most landlords, but not generally to BAA plc. This early indication of difficulties galvanizes both landlord and tenant to pool their knowledge in a joint effort to find creative ways to overcome the problems.

In order to measure success and to provide vital management information to retailers, in 1991 BAA plc designed and started operating a retail customer service monitoring research system. Four thousand five hundred customers are surveyed every month on all aspects of their retail experience including such issues as staff helpfulness, cleanliness, quality and value. This research has proved to be statistically robust with clear logical trends being recorded which can be acted upon by retailers and landlord alike.

Price monitoring

Having made commitments regarding competitive pricing, it was necessary to carry out extensive surveys to ensure BAA plc's claims were being met. Twenty-four pricing surveys are now carried out every year around the country, covering all key product areas so that competitiveness can be benchmarked.

RESULTS OF THE STRATEGY

It is interesting to see if the strategy has been successful by looking at some of the key indicators:

Retail space

Figure 11.1 illustrates how retail space grew between 1990 and 1997 through the development of carefully designed and planned retail areas in every major airport terminal. Each terminal at Heathrow and Gatwick now has the critical mass of space needed to give the customer the choice and retailer competition required by the strategy.

Sales and income

Over the same period, retail sales have grown by 85%. Clearly, growth of this magnitude could not have been achieved without the addition of a substantial amount of space, but it was the comprehensive customer focused strategy that enabled the opportunity to be exploited. Over the same period, net income grew by 83%; slightly down on the sales growth because of the anticipated cut in margin.

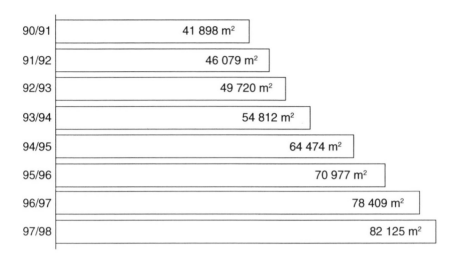

Figure 11.1   Growth of retail space at BAA plc airports

Customer service

High growth is only sustainable if achieved through customer satisfaction rather than, as had been the case, through pressure on margins and customer dissatisfaction.

Figure 11.2 highlights how value-for-money satisfaction scores have improved between 1990 and 1996. The changes are not dramatic but they are moving in the right direction; public perception is difficult to change and to some extent the cynicism of the late 1980s has not been eliminated. Nevertheless, bearing in mind the continuing poor quality of retailing at some airports around the world, this should be no surprise.

The lesson, in setting any strategy, is to be patient but persistent in attempting to change opinion and attitudes and thereby grow revenue.

Range and choice

The number of concessionaires has grown from 30 in 1988 to 200 in 1997. Competition and choice of outlet have grown dramatically in every key product area.

Press reaction

After years of adverse publicity characterized by stories about 'rip offs', press comments now are almost entirely favourable.

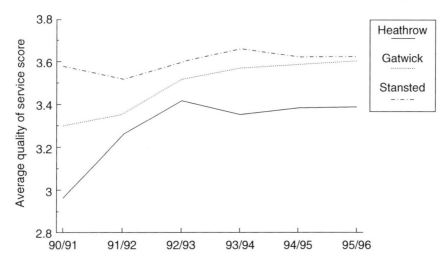

Figure 11.2   Retail value for money: average Quality of Service Monitor (QSM) scores (Source: BAA plc QSM)

Retail environment

The development of carefully planned retail areas improved the general environment for all passengers, whether shoppers or not. This in turn increased their propensity to spend.

Concessionaire relationships

These cannot easily be measured quantitatively, but a spirit of co-operation and trust undoubtedly exists between BAA plc and its concessionaires, helped considerably by the ability of BAA plc retail managers to talk knowledgeably about their partners' businesses.

A landlord's failure to understand the businesses they are hosting can be a major source of tenant frustration. Chris Baumann, the Deputy Chief Executive of Bally, commented:

> Other landlords often seem to have no clue about retailing and don't show any interest either.[2]   (Chris Baumann, Deputy Chief Executive, Bally, Uk, 1996)

and Steve Lemack, the Director of European Operations of Sunglass Hut, noted that:

> Other airport operators and mall landlords virtually ignore or at minimum give lip service to the average customer. BAA makes the customer's needs and satis-faction a major focus. They have created successful shopping environments and insist that the retailers are maintaining services and pricing thus providing shop-pers with the confidence and satisfaction they require. All this helps the retailer grow their business and increase turnover and profits.[3]
>
> (Steve Lemack, Director of European Operations, Sunglass Hut, 1996)

ISSUES, PROBLEMS AND OPPORTUNITIES

The BAA plc retailing operation has probably taken customer focused property management as far as any organization has to date. It has generated many opportunities and some difficulties that have had to be overcome. Most aspects of the approach are applicable to the high street but the implementation and expectations may need to be adapted.

Applicability to the high street

Ignoring for the moment any lease versus concession issues, there are different physical, locational and geographical issues that arise when applying the approach to the high street.

While many of the broad principles can be applied in almost any circumstance, the BAA plc approach can only be replicated if the landlord has considerable control over the entire space within which its retail partners are located. This is particularly the case when the landlord becomes involved in marketing, third-party customer service and branding issues. Clearly a landlord with a mixed portfolio of single high-street shops would gain less from these elements of the approach while a shopping centre could apply all of them.

What is important, however, is that property managers consider their businesses from the shoppers' and retailers' points of view and establish strategies that reflect their wishes and not the perceived needs of other stakeholders such as owning institutions.

The BAA plc strategy has already been very successfully transferred both to airports overseas and into the development and management of designer outlet shopping malls. In the case of town centres, where properties are held by a variety of landlords, their ability to compete with out-of-town centres will increasingly depend on the town centre managers' ability to implement this approach. It is not essential to have concession agreements or turnover rents in place to benefit from BAA plc's philosophy but this partnership approach certainly helps by ensuring that the retailers' and landlord's interests coincide and that benefits from any initiatives flow to both parties more equitably.

This approach has raised other issues that may seem particular to airports but probably have parallels in the high street.

Sharing the pain

Any business may be affected by unforeseen circumstances. For example, Heathrow and Gatwick suffered a 25% drop in passenger numbers during the 1991 Gulf War. Because of guaranteed minimums (see Annex 1), most retailers quickly found themselves making losses. Although there was no contractual obligation to do so, BAA plc renegotiated almost all contracts in order to share the pain during the crisis. This reduced the company's income but it was an essential gesture given the partnership nature of the business.

This was not a purely philanthropic gesture, however; it generated trust that made it easier to let space in the future to established business partners, even in locations they would not normally consider. Similar circumstances could occur in the high street as a result of, for example, terrorism, out-of-town competition or changes in local access.

Margin structures

The concession percentage paid by any operator is very much affected by the margin structure prevalent in that operator's field of business. Although that is taken into account at the time of negotiation, subsequent and dramatic changes in the business, such as the abolition of the Net Book Agreement in the case of bookshops, may require a review.

This is not a problem with a traditional lease, assuming the retailer is generating sufficient profit to cover their costs, and in any case higher sales volumes generated by discounting will often enable the retailer to maintain the cash margin.

In the case of a turnover related contract, if the retailer's margin falls too far, they may end up selling at a loss (see Annex 2). In such a case, volume

'THE SKY IS THE LIMIT'

growth will not help, and will in fact make things worse. Again, the partnership approach leads to a negotiated settlement.

SUMMARY

BAA plc's approach has undoubtedly been a success. It is not a prescription for every landlord and property manager but, if there is a will to become more customer focused, it provides a menu of approaches, options and initiatives which can lead to more successful business partnerships and more successful businesses.

Annex 1   Concession agreements

A concession agreement provides a retailer with a 'licence to trade' and falls outside the Landlord and Tenant Act and is more usually used by department stores when awarding in-store concessions. A number of characteristics set it apart from traditional leases, even where turnover rents are used:

- *Short term*   Agreements tend to be for only three to seven years. They will be at the higher end of this range if the retailer has a more substantial capital investment to amortize.
- *No automatic renewal*   Contracts will usually be tendered or renegotiated on expiry. There is no right to renewal.
- *Easy termination*   There will usually be a break clause allowing either party to terminate the contract on six-months' notice, for any reason. This provides flexibility and, from the retailer's point of view, a relatively low-cost exit should performance be unsatisfactory.
- *Financial terms*   The retailer pays a percentage of turnover monthly in arrears. The percentage varies substantially, according to the margin structure of the market within which it operates. Bureaux de change pay low, single figure percentages while conventional shop units may pay anything from 10–30%. The flexibility of this approach is such that retailers selling a broad range of goods with very different margins may pay different percentages for different product categories. Different percentages can also be set for different levels of sales.

Underpinning this will generally be a guaranteed minimum payment which usually represents 75–85% of the anticipated income. This is triggered (also monthly) if sales drop below the level required to pay the sales-driven rental. This prevents weak retailers from buying their way into sites and protects the landlord's income stream.

- *No extras* BAA plc does not levy retail service charges or marketing charges and pays rates. This provides a very clean agreement that minimises areas of potential conflict.
- *The incentive* The incentive to provide a high quality environment and to market it effectively comes from the financial structure of the agreement which ensures that any action that benefits the retailer through growing sales, will also benefit the landlord.

Annex 2

The figures given below are fictitious, but illustrate the different effects margin structures have on concession agreements and leases. The example hypothesizes a bookshop with a turnover of £1 million per annum, a gross margin of 50% and property costs (rent or concession fee) of £350 000. Its gross profit after rent is £150 000 per annum.

The abolition of the Net Book Agreement then leads to an increase in the sales volume of discounted books, but a reduction in their margin to 33%. It can be seen that in the case of a traditional rental agreement, sales volumes have grown faster than margins have declined, that the rent is fixed and that the retailer's profit actually grows.

Before abolition of Net Book Agreement

	Lease	Concession agreement
Total book sales revenue	£1 000 000	£1 000 000
Cost of sales	£ 500 000	£ 500 000
Rent	£ 350 000	£ 350 000*
	£ 850 000	£ 850 000
Retailer's gross profit after rent	**£ 150 000**	**£ 150 000**

After abolition of Net Book Agreement

	Lease	Concession agreement
Full price sales revenue	£ 900 000	£ 900 000
Cost of sales	£ 450 000	£ 450 000
	£ 450 000	£ 450 000
Discounted book sales revenue	£ 300 000	£ 300 000
Cost of sales	£ 200 000	£ 200 000
	£ 100 000	£ 100 000
	£ 550 000	£ 550 000
Rent	£ 350 000	£ 420 000#
Retailer's gross profit after rent	**£ 200 000**	**£ 130 000**

* Concession fee based on 35% of sales of £1 000 000
# Concession fee based on 35% of sales of £1 200 000

In the case of a concession agreement the landlord's income grows at the expense of the retailer's profitability. This is because the margins on discounted books are no longer sufficient to support a concession fee of 35% and the retailer is losing money on these sales. Unless terms are changed, the retailer would therefore be tempted to stop selling discounted books, with a consequential reduction in customer services, sales and concession fees.

Notes

1. Barry Gibson, Group Retail Director, BAA plc, internal communication 1996.
2. Chris Baumann, Deputy Chief Executive, Bally, UK, personal communication 1996.
3. Steve Lemack, Director of European Operations, Sunglass Hut, personal communication 1996.

12 American Case Studies

The commercial property markets of the USA and the UK exhibit many differences, the UK tending to have higher rents and longer lease terms and the US having a greater understanding of the need to satisfy tenants.

On the whole, property businesses in the USA have a more customer focused approach than those in the UK. The purpose of this chapter is to describe how three managers of property, based in the USA, are using the six Building Blocks in their day-to-day work. The lessons are not new ones but lend support to forward-thinking companies in other parts of the world in their quest for value and for excellence in customer service.

Table 12.1 shows the companies that best illustrate the use of the Building Blocks. Some companies appear in more than one category, which makes sense as a company committed to success in one area is likely to achieve success in many areas.

BLOCK 1   DEFINING THE CUSTOMER

The definition of the customer has changed surprisingly recently in the US commercial property industry. Previously, most property managers looked

Table 12.1   Use of the Building Blocks

Building Block	Company
1. Defining the customer	Insignia Commercial
2. Researching what the customer wants	LaSalle Partners
	The Lipsey Company
3. Creating a mission for the organization	Insignia Commercial
	The Lipsey Company
4. Leadership, empowerment, training and communication	Liberty Property Trust
5. Process improvement and information management	Insignia Commercial
6. Measuring success and benchmarking	LaSalle Partners

"TURNING THE CORNER"

at the owner that hired them as the customer. Now, in an effort to improve tenant retention, the owners themselves are placing more emphasis on the tenant and encouraging their property managers to do likewise.

Insignia Commercial is one of many property management firms that realize the importance of treating tenants as valued customers where good service and value lead to higher levels of retention. Insignia provides management and leasing services to more than 450 commercial properties with 9.9 million m^2 of space. It believes that focusing on fulfilling and surpassing the needs of tenants leads to improved asset performance; in other words, customer service is the means to a financial end.

Insignia has a clear belief: '*Customers do not make our jobs difficult, they make them possible.*' The company therefore created a three-step process to develop good relations with tenants right from the start. This is not rocket science but demonstrates a confident approach even to the simple process of the arrival of a new tenant:

- Step one covers activities before a tenant moves in, including initiating personal contact at hand-over and describing information that will be important to the tenant, such as the scheduling of janitorial services. At this point a personalized welcome sign for the main lobby of the building is also arranged.

- Step two starts on the move-in day, when property managers make personal contact, inquire about special needs, and schedule a time to introduce the management and maintenance team.
- Step three covers the first week when property managers again visit the tenant, sometimes present a welcome gift and answer questions.

It is simple but effective and shows the new tenant that their property manager cares. Tenants feel welcomed, comfortable and knowledgeable about the property management staff; just the right sort of start to a new relationship.

Insignia also responds to its other customer or stakeholder, the owner. As explained later, Insignia instituted standard operating procedures, called Best Practices, and field audits to ensure consistent high quality service to both owners and tenants.

BLOCK 2   RESEARCHING WHAT THE CUSTOMER WANTS

LaSalle Partners Management Limited, an international real estate services firm founded in 1968 and based in Chicago, found a productive approach to research. LaSalle provides investment advice, investment management, strategic planning and transaction services for more than 1.95 million m^2 of space. In its capacity as manager, not owner, LaSalle recognized the potential conflict between what owner-clients wanted and what tenants desired. Robert Best, the company's Vice-President, commented:

> A property management firm is in a kind of sandwich between two entirely different client bases, first the owners and second the tenants.[1]
> (Robert Best, Presentation on Managing Real Estate Course, 1996)

Owners want the best money-making deal and tenants want as many services as they can get at the lowest cost. The property manager keeps the balance.

LaSalle therefore undertakes regular surveys of both owners and tenants. The information from owners helps LaSalle deliver a better level of service to them and the tenant research is used to ensure better tenant responsiveness. The occupier research is also communicated to the owners and this facilitates much better understanding about the reasons why the managers are recommending a particular course of action. In this way a research-based approach is adopted which in the short term meets tenants' needs and in the longer term delivers financial success to the owner.

For example, in 1995 LaSalle surveyed 72 owners and analyzed the data on two levels. First, the survey provided property managers and corporate management with an understanding of the key issues affecting owner satisfaction. Second, LaSalle compared the results with occupier data from sources such as property inspections and audits to determine the relationship that existed between owner and tenant satisfaction. This resulted in the development of a corporate best practice programme and performance improvement plans to increase owner as well as tenant satisfaction.

LaSalle now uses an independent third party to telephone-survey tenants, and conducts an internal telephone survey for owners. It found that telephone interviews reap responses of 100%, especially in what is an over-surveyed sector. To supplement this research LaSalle holds annual focus group sessions for its 2000 tenants and, according to Best, 'This is always an eye opening experience and the sessions prove extremely effective.'

The Lipsey Company, based in Florida and run by Mike Lipsey, specializes in helping those in the real estate business to prepare for the future. Lipsey presents 250 programmes annually to corporate real estate executives from all sections of the industry and has developed a simple five-step process to ensure that real value is gained from a focus group.

- First, it sends a memo to all participants explaining what it is doing, why it is doing it, and how it works. In the memo, staff are encouraged to be candid and forthcoming.
- Second, it specifies groups of no less than four, and no more than eight, with no supervisors in the same group as the people they supervise.
- Third, the session lasts no more than one hour and requires a trained facilitator who is also independent.
- Fourth, it prepares questions in advance that are relevant to the particular situation. The responses are taped for use in creating a report.
- Finally, after delivery of the report, Lipsey encourages management to respond to what it hears, the starting point of which is a memo thanking employees for participating.

Their course catalogue states:

For a thorough analysis, The Lipsey Company will interview all members of staff, from top to bottom, in separate sessions designed to group various levels together. This provides an environment of camaraderie and a forum in which the participants can openly discuss issues, identify strengths and weaknesses and respond to questions.[2]

(Mike Lipsey, extract from The Lipsey Company's Consulting Services and Strategic Planning Course Catalogue 1996)

If well run, focus groups can be an invaluable source of high-quality, in-expensively-obtained information. But listening, understanding and reacting to questions and comments of customers, without rushing in with quick solutions, is an acquired skill.

In order to keep groups on track a successful facilitator will use well-crafted questions to defuse conflict and to handle persistent complainers or those who are contrary or try to dominate. The art is to channel the complainers' energy into finding a solution. Questions such as 'what three suggestions do you have for improving this department, or building, or process?' and 'what haven't I asked yet that I should have?' encourage the focus group to provide productive responses.

BLOCK 3   CREATING A MISSION FOR THE ORGANIZATION

The reasons for developing a mission have been covered in Chapter 4, but it is interesting to look at the experience in the USA.

Lipsey believes that a strong customer-focused corporate culture can and should be built around a mission statement that provides 'a sense of purpose, a sense of security and a sense of community'.

On one assignment, Lipsey evaluated a property management company's performance and found that the tenants were unhappy and the owner was unhappy. The main reason was that the property managers had no stated purpose and values; no mission. The company had become an everyday caretaker, preoccupied with answering maintenance requests and complaints about cleaning, and it had forgotten to be innovative and forward-thinking. It had forgotten to think about how it could add value and be of real worth to both owner and occupier. Management was in a rut.

The building's management and Lipsey held a focus group session with tenants to discuss what they wanted and a similar one to discuss what the owner wanted. It used open questions such as 'what things would you like management to do?' and 'what attracted you to the building?' At the conclusions of the sessions, Lipsey made a number of recommendations. One of them was that management had to find ways 'to revive it's competitive urges'; complacency had set in and without change the future was bleak. Management was encouraged to establish a process whereby the whole team could be part of an initiative to develop shared objectives, values and methods; in other words, a mission.

Each department – personnel, accounting, engineering – contributed to the mission statement which was intended to improve internal performance between departments:

> As a team, we will provide our associates at this firm with a superior service every day by ensuring a clean, comfortable and safe business environment through co-operation, planning and a positive attitude.[3]
>
> (The Lipsey Company, Mission Statement, 1984)

They wrote it; they now had no reason not to live up to it.

Insignia Commercial provides another example of how a mission can improve corporate practices. A mission statement is a first step; unless employees have helped create it and believe in it, it is worthless. Open discussion about the issues supported by training is therefore needed. Insignia's statement,

> To be recognized by the real estate industry, our clients, stockholders and parent company as the premier service-oriented real estate organization in the USA,[4]
> (Insignia Commercial, Mission Statement)

is supported with training. The company went as far as developing a corporate 'university' to help employees understand the company mission, values and processes.

Training programmes need to be designed with sensitivity so as to match the different skills, backgrounds and cultures of the participants. In the first part of Insignia's training participants looked at the mission statement and memorized the first sentence. Then the employees formed groups of four or five. Lipsey asked the groups to discuss and answer the question 'what prevents you from achieving this mission?' Four minutes later, the groups' responses included playing telephone tag, not enough technology, not enough training, too many staff meetings, and mixed signals from management.

Lipsey then gave the groups another four minutes to answer the question 'what three or four productive things can you do to be successful this year?' The employees pinpointed several things that, if done without any distractions, would support the mission and make them successful.

He then asked 'which of the two lists occupies your time?' Obviously it was the time-waster list. Insignia's employees thus accepted the challenge to change the way they operated so that maximum time could be spent on what really mattered, the customer.

Missions are valuable in motivating groups of people but they have little impact without having a personal as well as a corporate relevance. At Insignia, members of the team developed individual mission statements that they could place on their desks and read each morning to keep on track. By keeping a personal mission statement that mirrored the corporate statement, each individual felt like a part of the whole and contributed more, and more effectively.

In order to maintain predictable processes that help deliver the mission's objectives, Insignia has created eight three-ring binders of user-friendly policies that explain and support its mission. The information provided gives specific support on how to achieve the mission and how processes should be used to achieve the service objectives. The end result is a management team with clearly-focused members whose shared objectives and values can be met through efficient, well-understood processes that add value to tenants and owners alike.

BLOCK 4   LEADERSHIP, EMPOWERMENT, TRAINING AND COMMUNICATION

To achieve corporate excellence, staff require training, motivation, and reward. It is not what you do, it is how you do it and who does it.

At Liberty Property Trust of Malvern, Pennsylvania many best practices revolve around its employees, and the company believes that leadership and communication skills of employees are what make the difference. Liberty takes each part of Building Block 4 to heart and the company's attitude of respect towards its employees is evident throughout its operations. Liberty uses great care in selecting employees, it trains and empowers its staff, and then uses a systematic approach to communication.

When taking on employees, Liberty involves several people in the selection process. Existing staff usually sit in on the interviews and participate in the decision-making process. This gives everyone a sense of involvement in the corporate culture, and lets them know their ideas count. This is just one small, but important way, that Liberty encourages its employees to take on wider roles.

In selecting candidates, Liberty places a high priority on an individual's ethics as well as enthusiasm. Employees who join Liberty's team often do so with more confidence because they know that their selection was made by consensus and not just by the personnel manager. Additionally, Liberty employees find that once they are employed, they are treated with respect. The golden rule that you treat others as you wish to be treated yourself is very much a part of the corporate culture of Liberty.

In 1995, Liberty created a new corporate structure that was designed to provide better customer service and to be the key to its tenant retention programme. The new approach for improving customer satisfaction utilized teams for property management, maintenance, leasing administration, and sales. This team approach to its front-line service staff has been instrumental in improving Liberty's tenant retention programme. Internal communication has improved within Liberty and also with the tenants. Albert Kraft, the company's Vice-President, noted:

> We feel it is very important for each person on the team to develop a personal relationship with their counterparts. By getting to know and understand each other better, the team will increase their two-way communication. The better we get in improving communications, the stronger we will become as a group. The communication issue is the key to becoming a seamless organization.[5]
>
> (Albert J. Kraft III, Liberty Property Trust, 1997)

To ensure the team approach worked effectively, the firm then created a systematic approach to communication. Because there were so many people involved, a formalized communication process was critical in preventing important information from being overlooked. Scheduled on a regular basis, senior executives, regional managers and vice-presidents of sales meet once or twice a week. Information from the meetings filters down the ranks via the vice-presidents, who head up the teams.

In addition, there are twice-weekly meetings of staff in different disciplines, including property management, maintenance, engineering, accounting and administration. As they work in portfolio teams, they do not normally come into contact with others of their discipline every day and these meetings provide them with an opportunity to share ideas, problems and solutions. The team set-up definitely increased productivity for Liberty, and Albert Kraft commented:

> Setting up the team approach has been extremely effective. By using this approach, no single person has complete control, and each idea is considered. The team members feel a sense of ownership about their portfolio and this helps propel them to go the 'extra mile' to serve our customers.[6]
>
> (Albert J. Kraft, Liberty Property Trust, 1997)

The bottom line is that people are more productive when they feel they are in the know, that their thoughts are respected, and their efforts valued.

In addition to improved morale, which is difficult to quantify, the firm can measure success in its greater retention of tenants. As evidence, Liberty points to 30 tenants that have stayed more than 12 years.

BLOCK 5   PROCESS IMPROVEMENT AND INFORMATION MANAGEMENT (IM)

A process is unlikely to be cost-effective and efficient if it is not supported by high-quality management information provided through the use of up-to-date technology.

Insignia places great emphasis on process improvement and IM and has blended the two with a program called Envoy which links more than 400 properties across the USA through a sophisticated management information system.

Easy to use and trouble-free information systems are essential and that is why Insignia has established an IT help desk to resolve program, system, hardware, and printer problems promptly. Employees do not call a member of the IT staff directly but report problems to a user-friendly help desk, giving as much information as possible about the problem. The help desk solves minor problems over the telephone or commits itself to responding within two hours.

To achieve consistency of approach across locations, Insignia has put its eight best practice binders, representing thousands of policies, on-line through Envoy. Staff can 'hot link' quickly and gain access to best practice on a range of issues such as policies, standards and forms. High levels of real estate management are achieved through continuity and consistency of processes, leading edge technology, cost-effective communication and team work.

BLOCK 6   MEASURING SUCCESS AND BENCHMARKING

LaSalle places strong emphasis on statistical measurement of its progress and success in customer satisfaction and quality. With the motto of '*if you can't measure it, it doesn't exist*', measuring success has become an integral part of LaSalle's management practices and a challenge in every part of the operation.

LaSalle had taken its quality improvement programme seriously, and as an indication of its emphasis on quality in 1991 it decided to apply for the coveted Malcolm Baldridge Award. When LaSalle began the exhaustive process of filling out the 70-page-plus application form for the award, however, it discovered that its internal systems were not producing nearly enough measurements to meet the high standards required to apply for the award. In response, LaSalle made the commitment to establish a comprehensive qualitative and quantitative measurement system covering all aspects of the business. The project was aimed at trying to give more precise meaning to all its quality efforts. The firm started to create specific, measurable systems to quantify its successes, which became the forerunner of benchmarking for LaSalle.

With the goal of treating its tenants like guests, the way a fine hotel treats its customers, LaSalle has succeeded in developing practices that provide high levels of customer service and quality and, importantly, the system to measure its success. LaSalle puts an emphasis on people, support and systems. The firm provides 'on-demand' knowledge to its individual property managers with a central staff group that provides expertise in technical, safety and environmental areas. The company understands well what information is central to ongoing quality improvement. LaSalle commits the resources for technology to prove the information through the use of e-mail for messages and exchanges of reports and information. The goal is to keep everybody current and provide quick access to the information they need. Robert Best noted:

> We are committed to provide on-demand knowledge to keep our service level high; there are infinite possibilities to use technology to improve service. We would be operating blind without it.[7]
> (Robert Best, Presentation on Managing Real Estate Course, 1996)

Through its continuous improvement efforts, LaSalle has determined that the kinds of questions and format of questions can make a difference in the usefulness of the information gathered. LaSalle has concluded that questions with a 'yes' or 'no' answer simplify measurement and stimulate positive management action. Also, by making surprise property inspections at least twice yearly, regional managers can collect large amounts of useful data. They use a checklist with basic questions that have 'yes' or 'no' answers. The inspectors answer simple, objective questions such as 'when walking into the lobby, was there any visible dirt?' These kinds of random inspections provide qualitative information about performance as well as valuable information about correcting deficiencies. Additionally, they serve as a motivating force for managers. The managers tend to keep service at the highest possible level because the inspections are unscheduled, and they do not want to be found with their guard down.

Although LaSalle is pleased with its progress in measuring success, it has yet to find a good, competitive benchmark for the items it measures. Even though commercial real estate professionals recognize that benchmarking is important to the industry, the actual practice is not yet widespread or standardized in any form that could be adapted easily by LaSalle.

Trade associations such as the International Facilities Management Association and the Building Owners & Managers Association have started to provide some benchmarking data for commercial real estate and most definitely will provide more in future. Publications such as *Business Process Benchmarking: Finding and Implementing Best Practices*, *Benchmarking: The Search for Industry Best Practices*, and *Managing the Future: Benchmarking Compensation Trends in Commercial Real Estate*, are examples of recent publications that put the knowledge of top companies at your fingertips with practical steps to benchmarking, and illustrate why benchmarking is an essential part of good business. Because LaSalle considers itself as a leader within the industry, and as there is insufficient industry data available, the company believes that establishing its own internal standards is probably the best approach to benchmarking at present.

CONCLUSION

Best practice in the USA adds weight to the six Building Blocks approach and it is interesting that the case studies bring out a common theme. Each of the three companies and Lipsey followed a three-step process; they questioned, they listened and then they created a systematic approach. The process for creating a customer focused business works in all of the six Building Blocks, from researching a customer's needs to developing best practice.

Notes

1. Robert Best, Vice-President, LaSalle Partners Management Limited, Presentation at Managing Real Estate Course at Massachusetts Institute of Technology, April 1996.
2. Mike Lipsey, The Lipsey Company, extract from The Lipsey Company's Consulting Services and Strategic Planning Course Catalogue 1996, p. 23
3. The Lipsey Company, Mission Statement 1984.
4. Insignia Commercial, Mission Statement.
5. Albert J. Kraft III, Vice-President, Liberty Property Trust (1997) internal staff meeting.
6. *Ibid.*
7. Robert Best, Vice-President, LaSalle Partners Management Limited, Presentation at Managing Real Estate Course at Massachusetts Institute of Technology, April 1996.

13 Towards the Future

The first objective of anyone in business is to ensure the sustainability of the enterprise; without that there is no future. This can only be achieved by a company remaining profitable and profitability is the product of a business that is competitive. It follows that the competitive business is the one that adds value, continuously, to its customers and indeed to its business partners.

With the focus on business sustainability, it is interesting to consider trends for the future against the background of today's property management industry.

TENANTS AS CUSTOMERS

The logic of valuing customers is as applicable to the property industry as to any other, but for reasons of history property owners have not, with few exceptions, recognized the need to run customer focused businesses. This has, in part, been due to the traditions of the industry and to the way the law has been used by both landlords and tenants to resolve disagreements. This route of legal recourse has been used extensively by the property industry, in a way that many other industries, seeking to build business partnerships, would find unattractive. Nevertheless, this combative approach is not one that is the exclusive reserve of property; it is a wider problem. The RSA Inquiry *Tomorrow's Company: The Role of Business in a Changing World* noted that:

> The climate in which companies operate should enhance not hinder their competitiveness. However the UK culture supports adversarial rivalry rather than genuine competitiveness. Our institutions, including the law and parliament, have historically been adversarial in character. In business terms, this adversarial heritage is a costly inefficiency: our appetite for confrontation and conflict is wasteful.[1]   (RSA, 1995)

The ability of any company to survive if it has costly, inefficient and wasteful practices is doubtful and in any event the likely trend is that tenants will increasingly be in a position to demand change in the relationship with their space suppliers. Tenant demands and economic necessity are likely to drive property owners to adopt a customer focused approach.

A significant number of corporate takeovers are completed each year. Yet small organizations are also flourishing in many sectors where the entry barriers are low and where knowledge and information, not capital investment, are the key. The change over the last couple of decades to fast moving markets with ever decreasing product cycles and increasing consumer demands calls for greater flexibility and to 'be big but act small'. Alan White, the Director: Group Property of BT, commented:

> Powerful technology also means that small ... businesses can join together as 'virtual corporations' to offer a complete menu of services, similar to large organisations. This is an important development which gives small operators considerable competitive advantage over larger corporations.[2]
> (Alan D. White, extract from speech, KPMG Business seminar on Workplace and Workstyle Efficiency, 1996)

The property industry could therefore be faced with an increasing number of large organizations, with strong buying power, demanding more flexibility. There could also be a large number of smaller businesses with less certain futures demanding the same. Their needs, and hence the customer service theme of this book, will be paramount.

INTERNATIONAL COMPETITION

International competition breeds competitiveness, and particularly during the latter part of the 20th century companies have had an increased ability to operate across borders. By its very nature, the property industry has not been international; locations have not been transferable across national borders. This has produced somewhat insular property businesses in different countries, each one unfamiliar with international competition.

But industries are being forced to change and international competition is one of the drivers. National industries are no longer insulated from international competition. Trade barriers are being removed around the world and design in one country and manufacture in another is commonplace. This means that all organizations and their suppliers will have to find ways of meeting the challenges of remorseless global competition.

Studies indicate that those industries which have successfully integrated to achieve world-class performance are those which have been influenced strongly by international competitive pressure. For example, the automotive, aerospace, consumer durables and electronics industries have all made major improvements to products and in their delivery. This seems to be because the products can be manufactured and sold across borders and hence the opportunity for economies of scale become a primary drive for improvements. Those opportunities, because of the fixed nature of land, have not been open to property owners.

Property owners of tomorrow will need to become more international if they are to keep up with the strategies and aspirations of their customers.

These occupiers will look for similarity in quality of space wherever they operate, and will look for the flexibility of lease length available almost everywhere outside the UK.

As companies drive for improved performance in occupancy costs, they will be assisted by advances in technology which now make it quite possible to operate a business, not from one large headquarters building in one country, but from a series of facilities around the world. The location of these will be dependent, in part, on occupancy costs. Who would have thought that a major Swiss company could base a vital part of its organization in India, but Swissair has done just that by basing its finance accounting division and frequent flyer database administration programme in Bombay where high-quality staff and low costs add value to the airline. Other examples are British Airways plc (BA) which is transferring part of its accounting operations to Bombay because wage levels are one-fifth of those in Britain, and British Telecommunications (BT), which uses Indian software developers.

To companies such as Swissair, BA and BT, global competition is a natural part of their business challenge; tomorrow's landlords will actively assist such companies to improve their competitiveness in a spirit of true partnership.

FOLLOWING THE CUSTOMER

Perhaps landlords of the future will join other industries and produce their product where their customers want it. This would mean moving away from the somewhat hit-and-miss approach to speculative development, to one where the product follows the customer. An example of a company taking this approach is Regus which operates fully-serviced business centres. Mark Dixon, Managing Director, said that:

> The expansion of Regus is being customer-driven as the Company has many blue chip multi-national clients that require serviced office space in locations where Regus does not currently have a business centre. Regus is, therefore, planning to expand initially into locations which are attractive to its existing client base.[3]   (Mark Dixon, Managing Director, 1996)

Business centres are designed to cater for small and medium-scale occupations, but major companies sometimes set up project teams of up to 150 people for periods as short as 6 months. BT is one such company and is considering setting up Space Clubs with other corporations to provide this large scale, flexible space around the UK.

Property owners will need to choose between remaining local or national businesses, meeting some of the needs of their tenants, or taking the opportunity to grow profitability by meeting customer evolving needs on a worldwide basis.

A BUSINESS, NOT AN INCOME STREAM

In the past the property development industry has seen its product as the building, and its customer as the purchasing financial institution. In future, the customer will be the occupier and the product will be the space and facilities required for occupiers. Financial institutions have on the whole been fair weather friends to the property industry, understandably moving to other investments at low points in the property cycle. If property management is to be run as a business, not as a stream of investment income, then investment purchasers will also need to change in character and learn the skills necessary to run a property management business competitively. Stephen Bradley, of DEGW, has said that:

> If we accept that investment in land and buildings for office use is not an attractive destination for institutions to invest our pension and insurance funds, then can an alternative investment vehicle be found in companies who, like hotel and leisure operators, create value by the active management activities for business occupiers? The need is for broad-based entrepreneurial activity, not for conventional property development.[4]   (Stephen Bradley, The Workplace Forum, 1996)

The recession may have permanently changed how occupiers view their property. A long lease was seen as a way of securing occupancy but is now viewed as a potential liability. Industries may well start to think of property as just another consumable; something to be used and disregarded.

If this turns out to be the case, then serviced office operators will inevitably gain market share from those companies that specialize in creating long-term streams of income. Businesses will be willing to pay premium rents for an increasing number of their itinerant workers. It gives those companies the flexibility without the potential liabilities; they only take on what they need. Inevitably companies will increasingly resist being locked into leases that are longer than their industries time horizons which are getting shorter every year.

Tenants' desire for flexibility and value will tend to promote a move towards managing a concentration of property within a well-defined area, making it less costly to deliver the service standards that will surely become the norm in the future. Those who own business and industrial parks will be in a better position to compete than those with a scattered portfolio of properties.

Competition will be on the strength of each site's ability to offer its customers those things that have been discussed through this book, flexibility of terms, quality and flexibility of space, response standards and service assurance aimed at reducing disruption, social provisions such as cafés and meeting areas, and value added services and products.

DISCUSSION, NOT CONFRONTATION

The inability of landlords and tenants to work together in partnership causes a significant number of property related disputes which are time consuming, costly and damaging to relationships. These include applications to the courts to resolve obscure arguments on the construction of leases and large dilapidations claims. There is also a vast number of rent review arbitrations which increasingly assume all the characteristics, including the expense and time, of full blown litigation. Often the arbitrator's decision is appealed on a point of law.

Landlords have great experience at using the law to resolve differences, but even if a company has a good record at 'winning' cases, the effect of the litigation on the continuing relationship between the landlord and the tenant means there is no long-term winner. If landlords adopt a customer focused approach to their tenants then much of the conflict which, for reasons already mentioned, has been virtually inherent in the relationship should drop away. However, it is unrealistic to believe parties will never have differences. How then can these disputes be resolved without the time, cost and bitterness inherent in litigation and many arbitrations?

Alternative Dispute Resolution (ADR) may well provide the answer. It is a concept that originated in the USA and in recent years has gained many supporters in the UK. Its underlying philosophy is to bring the parties together at an executive level to reach a commercially sensible solution. This may not be the legally correct solution but will be the solution which meets the commercial aspirations of both parties. No losers just winners!

There are various forms of ADR ranging from mediation and conciliation to a mini-trial before a tribunal of executives from both parties. ADR is conducted in private and is generally not binding so either party may walk away until agreement is reached. The construction industry is increasingly using ADR and its wider application is now being recognized. Lord Woolf's final report on Access to Justice (1996) proposes that as a matter of procedure courts must encourage litigants to use ADR.[5]

Not all property disputes will be suitable for ADR. However, ADR's non-confrontational approach to disputes will help preserve the continuing relationship of supplier and customer essential to a successful property business.

POTENTIAL LEGISLATION

The property industry does not have a vote winning reputation, and as a result would gain little support from any government if it was considered to be acting unreasonably towards tenants. The passing of the Landlord & Tenant Covenants Act 1995, which largely established the system of privity of contract, was seen by many as 'anti-landlord', but was the government's response to strong lobbying from tenants.

Other Acts could follow, and the threat of further legislation was recently only averted by the industry agreeing to introduce a voluntary code of practice. 'Commercial Property Leases in England & Wales – Code of Practice' has the following aims:

- Improve practice in the business relationships between landlords, tenants and their advisors, particularly when a grant of a lease is being negotiated and at rent review.
- Encourage greater flexibility and choice through improved awareness of the alternative terms and conditions which may be negotiable.
- Promote greater openness and disclosure in the property market so that negotiations and the resolutions of disputes, particularly concerning rent review, are conducted with the benefit of more complete and accurate information.
- Ensure that businesses know more about how the market in commercial leases operates.[6]   (RICS, 1995)

The introduction of the code signals the government's continued interest in ensuring that landlords improve their performance. Robert Janes, the Minister for Planning, Construction and Energy Efficiency, commented:

I hope that the code will do much to bring about a better informed and more transparent market: one where all are fully aware of their rights and obligations. In particular, I hope that it will encourage flexibility in lease negotiations and greater transparency. As we announced last year, we intend to take a careful look at how well the code works in practice.[7]   (RICS, 1995)

The writing is surely on the wall. If landlords do not become more responsive to the needs of tenants then legislation will be introduced that will do the job for them. The impact on value of such legislation can not be quantified.

PROPERTY OWNER AS BUSINESS PARTNER

The property industry is a supplier to other industries and must respond as such by assisting companies to be competitive on a world scale. Continuous improvements in productivity are what companies are aiming to achieve. Landlords of tomorrow will wish to play their part by working in partnership with their tenants, to find ways of making their customers space more productive. Increased revenue is more likely to come from sharing increased value with the tenant, rather than simply from increasing rents.

The property owner of tomorrow may well use different performance indicators from today, ones that are better aligned to the objectives of the occupier's business. Measurement may not be based on rent per m², but rather on the annual occupancy costs per person, and there is likely to be more focus on ancillary occupancy costs such as those relating to the cost of the journey to work both in terms of money and the impact on the environment.

BT is an example of a company that faces stiff competition in its home market and overseas. It knows that if it is to remain competitive and successful only world class-occupancy costs will do. Alan White commented:

> What is clear is that we are looking for much more effective and efficient use of expensive office space, ideally utilizing the facility on extended time operation – perhaps 24 hours a day, but certainly double shift from 6am to 10pm.[8]
>
> (Alan D. White, extract from speech, British Property Federation National Conference, 1995)

BT is also taking active steps to drive down total occupancy costs. Office accommodation is the third largest cost to BT at just below £900 million per annum and between 1991 and 1996 the worldwide portfolio has reduced from just under 10 000 buildings to just over 8000. The company has made space reductions of 400 000 m² of offices and 800 000 m² of other space. The total of 1 200 000 m² is saving the company a staggering £300 million each year.

It is instructive that BT found its own answer to the problem of occupancy costs with its Workstyle 2000 programme where buildings have a range of facilities to meet the needs of a fast-moving business. Project work is an everyday part of the company's activities and so touchdown centres are provided for transient people between meetings, hot desks and flexible workstations, project rooms, quiet rooms, conference facilities and café and restaurant areas. Was the opportunity for the property industry to provide such a facility lost because property owners had continued their traditional approach of securing and collecting an income stream rather than anticipating the evolving needs of a major business partner? If so, an opportunity was lost.

In their drive for international competitiveness, occupiers need to use all the tools at their disposal to increase productivity. Landlords should be learning more about work culture, business processes and information technology so that they can help occupiers achieve productivity improvements in a spirit of true partnership.

Companies wanting to improve productivity often turn to experts in areas such as training or process improvement. Property owners can also help, not just by building more efficient buildings or by helping companies to occupy space more efficiently but by working with companies to help them utilize space in a way that helps change their culture, and hence competitiveness. Workstyle 2000 is an example of this:

We now know that our Workstyle 2000 programmes are substantially more effective at changing people's attitudes and productivity than training programmes have been in the past.[9]
(Alan D. White, extract from speech, UK Chapter of IDRC Europe, 1995)

Landlords should also be seeking ways to help occupiers achieve space productivity improvements and an example of this is a development by BAA Lynton plc at Heathrow. Dr Francis Duffy, the Chairman of DEGW, noted:

British Airways Compass Centre at Heathrow is an excellent example of space use intensification employed intelligently in a good quality speculative office building for a very specific purpose: the briefing of all BA aircrew operating out of Heathrow. What this means in practice is that a relatively small number of core staff permanently stationed in the Compass Centre are outnumbered by a tremendous flow of itinerant crew members. The operation is dependent upon huge IT resources and operates like a cross between a dealing room and the public parts of an hotel. Measured in terms of density and duration of use, of interaction, of information processed, the Compass Centre is a very productive building indeed – far more so than any conventional office.[10]
(Dr Francis Duffy, 'Flexible Working', 1995)

If landlords are prepared to act in a spirit of true partnership with tenants, then over time the rewards to both partners will be significant and the business of the landlord will certainly be more securely founded.

CUSTOMERS POINT TO THE FUTURE

The property industry will continue to exist; basić human needs such as comfort and the wish of people to work together should ensure that communal buildings in which people undertake work activities are, in one form or another, here to stay. The question is: 'which companies will be around to meet that need?' The answer is, those companies that have the vision to see the future.

The world is changing all the time but there are periods, such as the industrial revolution, when change takes place at a breakneck pace. It is at these times when traditional companies and indeed whole industries are at particular risk. It is a strange contradiction that, often, the most successful companies and industries are the ones at most risk. Success breeds complacency and a reluctance to do things differently. The British motorcycle manufacturing industry, at one time in a dominant world position, all but disappeared over the course of 20 years. Another example is the Swiss watch industry that missed out on a whole generation of manufacturing because of an inability to visualize the impact of quartz watches.

The property industry has some of the same traditional characteristics as the British motorcycle industry had but how can it ensure a different fate? The answer is with the customers; they are the experts and if listened to carefully, they will help guide company strategies to ensure that they are competitive and therefore sustainable.

FACILITIES MANAGEMENT

The property development industry's focus on the investment community as the customer has led to the curiosity that after a new building is completed it is handed over for occupation by a tenant that is asked to take on full responsibility for the facilities within that building. In a sense, the landlord, a professional in such matters, hands over responsibility to an amateur! Landlords that see their customer as the occupier would have the natural inclination to do the opposite; manage the facilities and in doing so add value to the tenant's business.

When old full repairing and insuring leases expire, tenants will probably say 'no' to renewal on similar terms; they will want to avoid becoming involved in a non-core activity such as facilities management. In the mea time, tenants with complex facilities are outsourcing the management but not, with few exceptions, to the property management industry. In most other industries such a role would be seen as an opportunity to add value to cu tomers and thereby strengthen their loyalty. Stephen Bradley of DEGW has said:

> The general response by the property industry to the opportunity to offer integrated services has been disappointingly slow. Facilities management has emerged as a distinct discipline in its own right, rather than as an extension of property management. There are some encouraging signs of knowledge transfer, in the high technology and communications sectors, between the disciplines of property management and facilities management disciplines, yet these are partly driven by the overlying trends of fixed cost reduction and outsourcing of support activities.[11]   (Stephen Bradley, The Workplace Forum, 1996)

Those landlords that are not taking responsibility for building services are missing another great opportunity to add value to their occupiers' businesses. After all, significant economies are available to large procurers of building services that in the main are not individual tenants. Building owners are in a much better position to use their knowledge and their buying power in a responsible way, to reduce the operating costs of buildings. This partnership approach has every likelihood of helping to build tenant loyalty and consequent landlord profitability.

ADAPTABLE ENVIRONMENT

As well as continuously seeking ways to help occupiers meet their business performance criteria, property owners will also need to help them support the changing working practices of their employees. Competitive pressures will force companies to drive up their productivity and one result will be fewer people doing more work. These people will be well rewarded and will expect an improved quality of life in the round.

Technology can make that link between higher productivity and an improved lifestyle and as a result home centred work will grow in scale. It was noted by Sir Iain Vallance at the CBI conference in 1994 that:

> The competitive edge will be gained by those companies that use the new technology to combine lifestyle and workstyle.[12]   (Sir Iain Vallance, 1994)

The prospect of people integrating their work and family life by spending more time working from home is a real one. People will be seeking a better quality of life by working flexible hours and spending less time commuting. This is another challenge to the property industry but one which will always be tempered by man's gregarious nature. Most of us are not psychologically attuned to working in isolation with only the mouse for company! These and other trends like it can either be viewed as a threat to the traditional property industry or an opportunity for property managers to contribute to the change and be part of it. As Stephen Bradley of DEGW has already noted:

> The challenge for developers, designers and providers of workplace facilities is to deliver and manage a range of adaptable environments which include physical settings appropriate for the varied cultural and environmental demands of different types of work.[13]   (Stephen Bradley, *The Architects Journal*, 1995)

As populations become more affluent, there will be increased pressure on the environment from more car users prepared to suffer longer journeys to work, compensated by the improved quality and facilities in their fou wheeled cocoons. Public transport must and will improve but will always find it difficult to compete with the personal flexibility and pricing that can be offered by a car. Can property owners play a part in cutting down car journeys?

With a clear focus on environmental sustainability, John Worthington of DEGW is developing concepts of integrated development planning around mass transport interchanges. This will enhance the logistical effectiveness of the movement of people, information and goods as well as minimizing the environmental impact. This theme of providing a range of workplaces at transport hubs may act as a counterbalance to the trend towards greater intergration of work and home environments.

With the coming of the industrial revolution, good planning dictated that homes and places of work should be separated. Now, improved environmental standards, the increased unattractiveness of commuting and the wish of people to spend more time at home may mean that the 21st century developer will be providing whole-life environments.

"HOT DESKING"

A working example of this philosophy is the development of Poundbury in Dorset, England. The Prince of Wales' Duchy of Cornwall has undertaken a development that recognises that we have became too car-dependent. The concept is to create a community where people can work and live in one place.

> The philosophy of Poundbury is not just about the architecture as is often thought. It is very much to do with the careful, detailed planning of an attractive, modern and pleasing place in which people can live, work, shop and play. Central to the Poundbury concept is that a new development of this size should include not just houses and flats, but also work places, shops, schools, leisure and community buildings – sensitively arranged, unlike most recent housing estates.[14]   (Duchy of Cornwall, 1996)

There appears to be growing agreement that the future holds some big changes. People will be expected to be more flexible in the way they work, and do more work at home or in temporary locations, facilitated by new technology. Part-time work and job-sharing will increase and people will have more than one career in their lifetime with greater periods of self-employment. The challenge for property owners will be to secure a place in this new world.

TECHNOLOGICAL ADVANCES

Technological advances will continue to change the requirements of occupiers to an extent that it is difficult to forecast today. Property owners that keep close to their occupiers will be best placed to see and plan for the changes that lie ahead. Stephen Bradley of DEGW put it succinctly when he said:

> The challenge for the providers and managers of workplaces is to face up to the challenges and opportunities of new technology, and to enable increased independence of the location where work tasks are performed.[15]
>
> (Stephen Bradley, *The Architects Journal*, 1995)

Technology is giving people the ability to be mobile, but at the same time, stay in touch. This means that many of the physical tasks that take place in the workplace are no longer necessary and the result will be reduced space requirements.

Technological advances can benefit both occupiers and owners, and one example of this is the move towards cordless technology. Research by Deloitte Touche, 'The Impact of Wireless Communications on Business in the 90s', found that:

> The benefits have been considerable for those companies that have implemented cordless office systems. Not only can office layouts be planned with much greater flexibility: the ability to contact employees easily wherever they are can markedly improve a company's responsiveness.[16]
>
> (Morgan Lovell, *The Cordless Office Report*, 1995)

Cordless systems is an example of a technological advance that can benefit occupiers and owners alike. Philip Ross, a Director of Morgan Lovell, commented that:

> The immediate short-term applications of the technologies are obvious: buildings with low slab-to-slab height and no raised floor, listed buildings, the presence of asbestos, temporary staff relocations, specialist teams deployed on client sites such as audit teams, and buildings on a short lease. The size of this market should not be underestimated. During the explosion of networked IT during the 1980s, the typical 1960s building with its low ceiling height did not allow for a raised floor to be installed. So 'old' buildings were demolished to make way for the high tech 80s environment. But cordless technology will make it possible, and indeed attractive to make use of older office stock.[17]   (Philip Ross, *The Cordless Offiice Report*, 1995)

Quality landlords of the future will be actively finding ways to utilize technological advances for the benefit of their tenants businesses.

INVESTOR EXPECTATIONS

Stock markets are often criticised for concentrating too much on a company's short-term performance and too little on its key drivers for long-term success. Not enough emphasis is placed on the softer issues such as leadership, training, community responsibility, and supply chain management and yet these are the things which will have a significant impact on a company's long-term competitiveness.

There are some signs of change and these are to be welcomed. Kleinwort Benson Investment Management has launched an Investment Fund that will invest in companies that adopt an 'inclusive' approach to management as recommended by the RSA Inquiry: *Tomorrow's Company*, and now expounded by The Centre for Tomorrow's Company. The Centre has been set up,

> to inspire and enable British business to compete with the world's best through applying the inclusive approach.[18]
>
> (Mark Goyder, Director, *News from the Centre*, 1997)

Companies being considered by the Tomorrow's Company Fund will be judged against a set criteria, described by Kleinwort Benson Investment Management in the following terms:

> Investment will be concentrated on those UK companies who are adopting an 'inclusive' approach in the management of their business. The 'inclusive' approach is a recognised, distinctive management philosophy identified by the RSA Inquiry into Tomorrow's Company. It sees a company's relationships with its key constituent groups as the main driver of competitive performance. Its key constituent groups are defined as customers, employees, suppliers, investors and the broader community. Inclusive companies develop a management process which maximizes performance from these relationships, with the objective of optimising competitive performance.[19]   (RSA Inquiry, 1995)

Kleinwort Benson believes that it has developed a distinctive investment process which allows the Trust to identify the companies most likely to produce sustainable business success. The process places particular emphasis on the creation of value through the maintenance of a healthy network of relationships, both within and without a company. Indeed, Kleinwort Benson have back-tested a representative cross-section of UK companies to establish whether there was a link between companies adopting an 'inclusive' approach and their share price performance. Interestingly, the model portfolio of companies adopting the 'inclusive' approach out-performed the FTSE-A All Share index by 16.7% for the period January to October 1996, and by 38.3% over the longer period from January 1993 to October 1996.

It will be interesting to see how the live fund performs, but it will certainly have the right ingredients for success. It is easy to see that if successful this approach could become the norm, and property owners will need to consider if they are well-placed to take advantage of such funding. The Chairman of the RSA Inquiry: *Tomorrow's Company* commented that:

> Those companies successful in the future will maintain a commitment to focus on shareholders and financial measures of success, but will also add per-

formance measures for the company's other key relationships: employees, customers, suppliers and the broader community.[20]

(Sir Anthony Cleaver, quoted in 'The Investment Opportunity', 1995)

THE REWARD FOR QUALITY

Perhaps the ultimate accolade that a landlord could receive from a tenant would be 'I am proud to occupy one of your buildings'. This pride would emanate out of good quality, service and value provided by the landlord, but also something more. Landlords of the future may only become profitable by focusing on the needs of their customers, but to sustain profits they must also be mindful of their wider responsibility to the community and in respect of the environment.

Community

Many landlords take their community responsibility seriously and others will need to in the future. Law and regulation used to be sufficient to enable a company to undertake its business activities but community endorsement will become a requirement in many situations. Earning this 'licence to operate' will be the mark of a quality company.

> According to the Ethics Resources Centre in Washington DC more than 60% of American companies and almost 50% of European companies now have some type of corporate community involvement programmes in place, and the number is growing.[21]
>
> (Suzman, Financial Times Business in the Community Supplement, 1995)

An example in the UK is Marks & Spencer which is a founder member of Business in the Community and encourages other companies to play an active part in their communities. Its community involvement includes community development and environmental programmes, health and care projects, and arts and heritage initiatives. For 1995/96, the total community involvement budget was £8.5 million, to which it donated £4.9m (Annual Report and Financial Statements, 1996).[22]

The property owner that can create a strong link between positive community involvement and its buildings may gain competitive advantage by attracting businesses keen to be linked to greater social responsibility. This linkage may well become more important to businesses in the future and, as with quality, something that they will be happy to pay a premium for. The RSA Inquiry: *Tomorrow's Company* noted that:

> Tomorrow's Company recognizes its interdependence with the community in which it operates. It develops leadership strategies which strengthen both the climate for business success and the community itself. Yesterday's companies stick to an insular view. They see the communities in which they operate as either a neutral factor in their success or a potential source of interference to be resisted.[23]   (RSA Inquiry, 1995)

Evidence already supports the premise that the business of the future will have to be not just a 'quality organization', but a caring one; one that is not only commercially successful and good for its primary stakeholders, but also sensitive to the needs of the community in which it operates.

Impact of new development

Many developers take great care to ensure that their buildings are of architectural merit and this is to be commended. Buildings after all take a relatively short time to put up but affect their environment for generations. Good architecture is a prerequisite of responsible development and is also good commercial sense.

The softer issues of development will become more important in such areas as incorporating art within architecture. Such an art policy recognises that tenants are not inanimate objects but individual people who have the right to expect that their working environment will be made as uplifting as possible. An art programme can also fulfil a developer's wider community responsibility by encouraging artistic talent to flourish. Who knows, commissions of today may be regarded as masterpieces tomorrow. Sandra Percival, Public Art Development Trust, has stated that:

> Art is one way in which we can strive to create socially and physically engaging surroundings; it can challenge our preconceptions in ways which make us better able to participate in the creation of a cultured and civilised society.[24]
> (Sandra Percival, Executive Director, Public Art Development Trust, 1996)

Environment

Property owners have sometimes been backward in coming forward as far as environmental issues are concerned, seeing more challenging standards as a threat to profitability. With a much wider understanding of the world's diminishing resources and the impact of pollution in all its forms, quality occupiers of space will in future reward landlords that set high standards in these areas. Landlords will be judged on their use of building materials from sustainable sources, on minimizing disruption to neighbours during construction, and on building designs that minimize energy use and emissions of pollutants. Again the RSA Inquiry *Tomorrow's Company* noted:

> Tomorrow's Company recognises the critical importance of achieving environmental sustainability in the interests of all stakeholders and accepts the challenge this poses. Yesterday's companies view environmental concerns as peripheral and react defensively when issues arise.[25]   (RSA, 1995)

CHANGE IS ON THE WAY

Owners' attitudes to occupiers began to change in the early 1990s when a vast oversupply of space in most sectors of the property market, first in the USA and subsequently in the UK, placed the occupier in a commanding position. Owners had to take account of tenants' wishes. It was, however, a somewhat grudging change of attitude and many people believe that the industry will be able to go back to its old ways when the supply and demand for accommodation are better balanced.

However, a few property owners have become committed to developing and maintaining a customer focus in providing and managing commercial buildings and accommodation. They see this as the means of building a long-term and, by definition, a profitable business.

BAA was the first company in the UK to adopt a customer focused approach to property management through the introduction of the Property Challenge, and it is interesting to see how three of the UK's largest property investment and development companies are starting to think in a refreshingly different way.

MEPC plc, in its 1994 report and financial statements, stated that:

> our mission is to respond to the business needs of our customers by delivering exceptional quality of service and, at the same time, endorsing a commitment to fair business practices which support responsible environmental standards.[26]
>
> (MEPC plc, 1994)

Ronald Spinney, Hammerson plc, in the group's 1995 annual report, said:

> At Hammerson we are committed to providing the best possible service to our tenants. In a competitive market-place, it is not enough simply to own the properties. We have to continually strive to enhance the service we provide to the group's tenants. By building on our excellent reputation in this area, we will increase our ability to attract and retain tenants.[27]
>
> (Ronald Spinney, Chief Executive, Hammerson plc, 1995)

In 1995, Land Securities plc, in its report and financial statements, stated:

> Our philosophy is based on the fundamental principles of first class location, strength of covenant, security of income and high quality specification. Our key strategy is to maximize the opportunities to add value by paying constant attention to the location, quality, composition and condition of our portfolio. This is achieved by carrying out refurbishments and new developments and by making acquisitions and sales at the appropriate times in the property cycle. Our aim is to provide shareholders with long-term sustainable growth in the form of a secure and increasing income together with capital appreciation.[28]   (Land Securities plc, 1995)

In 1996, Land Securities continued to be committed to providing shareholders:

> with long-term sustainable growth by a secure and increasing income, together with capital appreciation.

Importantly it had added:

> Our priority is to meet the needs of our tenants by providing the type of property, facilities, services and environment they require for the efficient operation of their businesses.

The Report went on to say:

> Above all, detailed attention to the management of our properties and the provision of high quality service to our tenants are fundamental to our future success.[29]
>
> (Land Securities plc, 1996)

When a major occupier of space such as British Telecommunications plc says that it would be prepared to pay a premium over current market rents to owners prepared to provide accommodation on terms that better match its business needs, then the property sector cannot afford to ignore the message (Alan D. White, extract from speech, Nacore Conference on International Site Selection, 1996).[30]

PROFIT THROUGH SATISFIED CUSTOMERS

The theme of this book is about landlords adopting a customer focused approach to property management. The proposition is that property owners that satisfy their customers and continuously seek to add value to their businesses will be more profitable than those that do not. In a fast-changing world, with global competitiveness becoming the norm, companies that do not adopt this new way of doing things will lose their competitiveness, and when this happens the very sustainability of a business is put at risk.

The last word should be from the RSA Inquiry *Tomorrow's Company*:

> By itself, financial performance does not gauge the overall health of the business. It neither defines competitive performance, nor measures the broader value created through product quality, speed of response and service. Companies which rely solely on financial measures of success are exposing their shareholders to unnecessary risk and denying themselves the opportunity to improve returns.
>
> Tomorrow's Company aims to retain and to develop new business with customers as part of a relationship which creates value for both parties. It seeks demanding customers who will help it drive innovation and competitiveness. Yesterday's companies see customers only as a source of revenue and profit, and sales only as transactions. They compete on price and are content with undemanding customers.[31]   (RSA, 1995)

The question for every reader of this book is, which do you want your business to be?

Notes

1. Royal Society of Arts (RSA) Inquiry (1995) *Tomorrow's Company: The Role of Business in a Changing World* (Aldershot: Gower).
2. Alan D. White, BSc. FRICS. MCR. Director: Group Property, British Telecommunications plc (BT), Extract from the Impact of Technology on Business Occupation (Speech, KPMG Business Seminar on Workplace and Workstyle Efficiency, London, February 1996).

3. Mark Dixon, Managing Director, Regus. Personal communication, November 1996.
4. Stephen Bradley (DEGW), 'Reinventing the Corporate Real Estate and Facilities Management Function', The Workplace Forum, May 1996.
5. Rt Hon Justice Woolf, *Access to Justice* – Final Report, July 1996.
6. Royal Institute of Chartered Surveyors Business Services (1995) *Commercial Property Leases in England & Wales: Code of Practice* (London: RICS). Reproduced with the permission of the Commercial Leases Group which owns the copyright.
7. Robert Jones MP, Minister for Planning, Construction and Energy Efficiency. (Inside endorsement to Commercial Property Leases in England & Wales – Code of Practice, December 1995). Reproduced with the permission of the Commercial Leases Group which owns the copyright.
8. Alan D. White, BSc. FRICS. MCR. Director: Group Property, British Telecommunications plc (BT), Extract from The Vision of the Office you Wish you Had (Speech, British Property Federation National Conference, February 1995).
9. Alan D. White, BSc. FRICS. MCR. Director: Group Property, British Telecommunications plc (BT), Extract from The Workplace Dimension (Speech, UK Chapter of IDRC Europe, December 1995).
10. Dr Francis Duffy, Chairman of DEGW, Accommodating Change, 'Flexible Working', November 1995.
11. See note 4.
12. Sir Iain Vallance, CBI Conference, March 1994. Quoted in 'Facilities Management' Management Guide no. 9, November 1995, p. 3.
13. Stephen Bradley (DEGW), *The Architects Journal*, 2 November 1995.
14. Poundbury Philosophy, Duchy of Cornwall, 1996.
15. Stephen Bradley (DEGW), *The Architects Journal*, 2 November 1995.
16. *The Cordless Office Report*, p. 59 Morgan Lovell, 1995.
17. Philip Ross, Director, Morgan Lovell. (*The Cordless Office Report* (p. 50) Morgan Lovell (June)) 1995.
18. Mark Goyder, Director, The Centre for Tomorow's Company, *News from the Centre – The Journal of the Centre for Tomorrow's Company* (p. 1), January 1997.
19. Kleinwort Benson Investment Management (June 1995) 'RSA Inquiry: Tomorrow's Company: The Investment Opportunity'.
20. Sir Anthony Cleaver, Chairman, AEA Technology plc (Chairman, RSA Inquiry: *Tomorrow's Company*), quoted in *The Investment Opportunity*, Kleinwort Benson Investment Management, June 1995.
21. Mark Suzman, Social Affairs Correspondent, The Financial Times Ltd, 'A Fine Act to Follow', Financial Times Business in the Community Supplement 1995, supported by KPMG.
22. Marks & Spencer plc, Annual Report and Financial Statements, 1996.
23. See note 1.
24. Sandra Percival, Executive Director, Public Art Development Trust, personal correspondence, November 1996.
25. See note 1.
26. MEPC plc, Report & Financial Statements, 1994.
27. Ronald Spinney, Chief Executive, Hammerson plc, Annual Report, 1995.
28. Land Securities plc, Report & Financial Statements, 1995.
29. Land Securities plc, Report & Financial Statements, 1996.
30. Alan D. White, BSc. FRICS. MCR. Director: Group Property, British Telecommunications plc (BT) Issues Affecting UK Site Selection and Corporate Real Estate (Speech, Nacore Conference on International Site Selection, San Francisco, July 1996).
31. See note 1.

Appendix: BAA plc Mission Statement

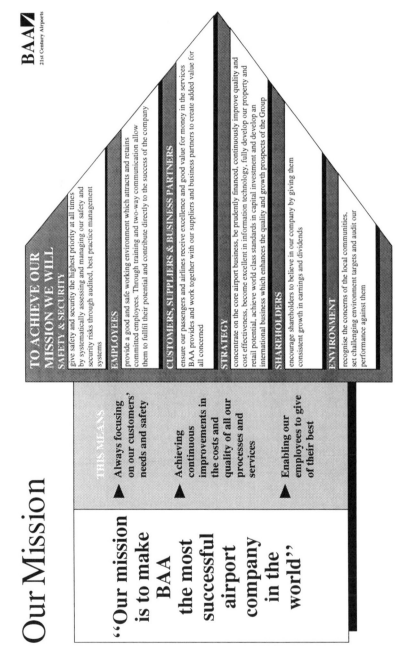

BAA
21st Century Airports

Our Mission

"Our mission is to make BAA the most successful airport company in the world"

THIS MEANS

▲ Always focusing on our customers' needs and safety

▲ Achieving continuous improvements in the costs and quality of all our processes and services

▲ Enabling our employees to give of their best

TO ACHIEVE OUR MISSION WE WILL

SAFETY & SECURITY

give safety and security the highest priority at all times by systematically assessing and managing our safety and security risks through audited, best practice management systems

EMPLOYEES

provide a good and safe working environment which attracts and retains committed employees. Through training and two-way communication allow them to fulfil their potential and contribute directly to the success of the company

CUSTOMERS, SUPPLIERS & BUSINESS PARTNERS

ensure our passengers and airlines receive excellence and good value for money in the services BAA provides and work together with our suppliers and business partners to create added value for all concerned

STRATEGY

concentrate on the core airport business, be prudently financed, continuously improve quality and cost effectiveness, become excellent in information technology, fully develop our property and retail potential, achieve world class standards in capital investment and develop an international business which enhances the quality and growth prospects of the Group

SHAREHOLDERS

encourage shareholders to believe in our company by giving them consistent growth in earnings and dividends

ENVIRONMENT

recognise the concerns of the local communities, set challenging environment targets and audit our performance against them

Index